specialist
sports cars

specialist
sportscars

THE GOOD, THE BAD AND THE UGLY OF A VERY BRITISH BREED

RICHARD HESELTINE

Haynes Publishing

First published in June 2001

A catalogue record for this book is available from the British Library

ISBN 1 85960 690 3

Library of Congress catalog card no 00-135912

Published by Haynes Publishing, Sparkford, Nr Yeovil, Somerset BA22 7JJ, UK.
Tel: 01963 442030 Fax: 01963 440001
Int. tel: +44 1963 442030 Fax: +44 1963 440001
E-mail: sales@haynes-manuals.co.uk
Web site: www.haynes.co.uk

Haynes North America Inc., 861 Lawrence Drive, Newbury Park, California 91320, USA.

Printed and bound in Great Britain by J.H. Haynes & Co. Ltd, Sparkford.

Most of the photographs appearing in this book have been supplied by the author and LAT.

Photographs have also been provided by Malcolm McKay and Simon Clay.

The TVR Tuscan V8 appearing on the front cover was kindly provided by Ian Massey-Crosse and photographed by Simon Clay.

Contents

Introduction

The Buckler, seen here trialing, was effectively the first true kit car, forerunner of the specialist sports car.

Britain's small cottage industry of specialist sports car manufacturers has become something of an institution, responsible for some of the most sublime machines ever to grace the asphalt – and also some of the most horrific. But what exactly constitutes a specialist sports car? There is no precise definition but, for the purposes of this book, it is any low-volume sports car produced by an independent player, ranging from such well-known and (relatively) well-funded operations as Lotus and TVR, to long forgotten minnows such as Dial and Butterfield.

The beauty of this under-appreciated arena of motoring subculture is the diverse and often bewildering array of marques and models, all of which provide an alternative to mainstream offerings. There has never been a shortage of dreamers and 'wannabe' motor moguls willing to risk everything in the hope of realising their visions of automotive heaven. Some are roaring success stories, while others shoot to the stars like a rocket, only to return to earth a scorched stick as they become last week's news. Some disappear into the ether before the ink on the press release has dried. But regardless of their merits or otherwise, classic specialist sports car have attracted a small adoring retinue the world over.

The industry's origins can be traced back to the efforts of Derek Bucker, a visionary who dreamed up the notion of offering sports cars in component form for budding racing drivers. That was in the late '40s, myriad other enterprising designers and copyists following in his wake. The new wonder material, glassfibre, undoubtedly had a great effect on the explosion of new manufacturers, the '50s 'specials boom' spewing forth an enormous variety of sporting chariots for budding DIY builders. Most of these were stark devices based on Ford Popular or Austin Seven running gear. The other, more telling reason for their success was the dearth of affordable, mass-produced sportsters.

The Martin was a typical example of the '50s Ford-based special.

John Haynes's early publications were a boon to early kit-car builders, covering Austin 750 ...

But the bubble soon burst as the decade drew to a close. The arrival of the Austin-Healey Sprite and the Mini put paid to many industrial stalwarts, while other better-funded concerns moved increasingly upmarket. And it was the '60s that saw the arrival of the true specialist sports car in the accepted sense, generally thoughtfully conceived, well-designed machines with brand-new parts, usually offered in component form to avoid purchase tax. But this situation did not last long. 1963 proved a watershed year, with then Chancellor Reginald Maulding cutting purchase tax on new cars by 50%, wiping out the tax advantage of kit cars in a stroke. Many companies went to the wall, others proved more hardy.

By the end of the '60s the movement had found its feet, with some of the better-established firms producing several hundred cars per year, many exported to America and elsewhere. But this prosperity could not last. The arrival of the fuel crisis in 1973, combined with the imposition of VAT and the three-day working week, effectively killed off the industry. Some marques weathered the storm, but most went the way of the Dodo.

This book aims to fill a significant void in the motoring book market. While some of the names featured already have texts dedicated to them, the majority do not, nor are they likely to. Unravelling the often conflicting stories, and tapping the memory banks of one-time industry insiders was a near impossible task, but somehow it has been made possible. I sincerely hope that you derive some pleasure from our efforts.

Acknowledgements

I owe a huge debt of gratitude to the following for their invaluable assistance in completing this book:

Mark Hughes and Steve Rendle of Haynes Publishing for their unflagging enthusiasm and tenacity in the face of continuous delays from the author in producing the goods. To Jon Pressnell whose idea this book was in the first place. Alastair Clements for doing his best to keep me sane and for (repeatedly) fixing my computer, and Chris Rees for letting me tap into his seemingly unfathomable depths of knowledge. To Peter Rix, Julian Kingsford-Booty, Tom Karen, Chris Lawrence, Dennis Adams, David Hopkins, Bob Hui, Martin Jamerson, Malcolm McKay, The Gilbern Owners' Club, the Clan Crusader Owners' Club, the Peerless & Warwick Register, and all those whom I've omitted to mention.

This book is dedicated to Julie-Anne

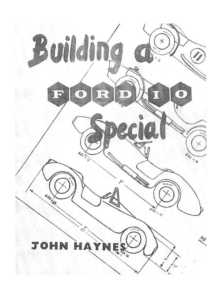

... and Ford 10 specials. Haynes Publishing is now the world's leading publisher of motoring books.

UYE 988

Berkeley

The Berkeley B65 was powered by a 328cc Excelsior twin, producing 18bhp. Stirling Moss predicted that the car had a future in competition after testing an example at Goodwood.

Berkeley B60	
Made	Biggleswade, Bedfordshire
Engine	Air-cooled, twin-cylinder 322cc 2-stroke
Construction	Fibreglass unitary
Top speed	60mph
0–60mph	19 seconds
Price new	£559

Success can be a fickle mistress. Just when you are surfing the mighty wave of achievement, the current changes and you nearly drown. Caravan manufacturer Berkeley Coachworks was at its zenith in the mid-'50s, its products comfortably outselling those of its rivals. Company principal Charles Panter then took the bold decision to build sports cars; a decision which, largely through no fault of his own, would cause the firm to drop to its knees. The reasoning behind the move was perfectly sound – caravan sales were largely seasonal, and Panter was keen to launch an additional product to keep his highly skilled workforce busy during the quiet winter months.

The move into automobile assembly followed a visit to Berkeley's Berkshire factory in the winter of '55 by maverick designer Laurie Bond. Famed for his crude but popular trikes, and rather less so for his idiosyncratic racing cars, Bond had approached several likely manufacturers with his vision of a small motorcycle-engined sports car, but found no takers. Panter, however, was receptive, reasoning that with all his years of experience with glassfibre, producing car bodies of the same material would pose no problem. A deal was negotiated in the spring of the following year, on the proviso that a finished prototype would be displayed at the October Earls Court Motor Show.

Bond and his small team made rapid progress. A melange of proven sports car design and non-conformist individualism, the prototype resembled a scaled-down AC Ace. The car's monocoque was constructed from only three major mouldings – a long, flat undertray that incorporated aluminium box-section sills, a nose section reinforced with alloy bulkheads, plus the tail segment. Power came from a chain-driven, 322cc Anzani two-stroke motorcycle engine mounted transversely, with suspension similar to Bond's hillclimb racer. At the

8

America was swift in adopting the Berkeley marque. Here Bill Harding negotiates the Esses at Virginia International raceway in May '58 in his B65.

back was a simplistic swing-axle and wishbones, the front end suspended by unequal length wishbones.

The Berkeley Sports (B60) made its show debut and proved one of the star turns, with the press clamouring for test drives. With an all-up weight of just 6.5cwt, the Lilliputian roadster could hold its own against most humdrum production saloons, despite its meagre engine capacity. An irregular supply of engines swiftly resulted in a change to a slightly hotter, but otherwise largely similar, 328cc Excelsior twin (this variant was known as the B65). Now with 18bhp on tap (a 20 per cent increase over the Anzani), the baby Berkeley could gallop to 60mph in around thirty seconds. Motor racing hero Stirling Moss track-tested one at Goodwood for the BBC's *Sportsview*, and predicted that the car had a future in competition, although reasoned that some drivers could have trouble adapting to the car's front-wheel-drive layout.

Buoyed by the good press, Bond and Panter pushed ahead with further developments. At the '57 Earls Court Motor Show, the Sports was displayed with a number of improvements, especially in body detailing, along with the new Sports Deluxe edition which was offered in open and fixed-head coupé configurations. This new variant bore several refinements over the standard model, including such niceties as fancy wheel trims and a tachometer. The biggest change was the adoption of two Amal carburettors. A further option, for the B90 variant, was a three-cylinder 492cc motor, developed especially for Berkeley by Excelsior, which churned out 30bhp at 5500rpm. Unfortunately, this warmed-over unit proved unreliable, causing innumerable warranty claims.

B65s proved immediately competitive on the track. Esteemed driver and entrant Count 'Johnny' Lurani fielded a three-car team at races all over Europe, taking class honours in the '59 Verona 12-hour endurance event among others, the squad including future Grand Prix star Lorenzo Bandini.

With the sporting family man in mind, Berkeley launched the Foursome in late-'58, which was essentially an elongated Sports with 492cc-twin power. In order to accommodate the rear bench seat, the wheelbase was extended by eight inches, and the car was widened by four inches. This model was to prove

The B60 made its debut at the '56 Earls Court Motor Show. Early publicity came from *The Daily Mail* which gave away six examples.

9

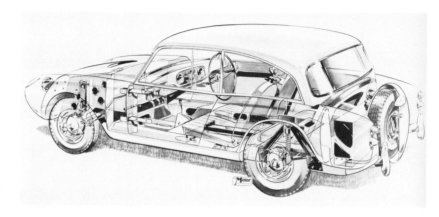

A cutaway of the B90 displays the compact dimensions and cramped cabin area. This variant used a 492cc motor developed by Excelsior.

short-lived, as the cramped cabin did nothing to woo customers: nor did the severe scuttle shake and body flex. Just 22 Foursomes were made, making this the rarest of all production Berkeleys.

Despite this momentary blip, the firm had a healthy customer waiting list. The demand for more power was answered with the introduction in March '59 of the 40bhp, 792cc Royal Enfield Meteor-powered B95. Essentially a B90, but with an elevated bonnet line to accommodate the new four-stroke lump, its new frontage incorporated Lucas headlights in place of the usual faired-in Wipac units. Though not exactly a vision of loveliness, this latest variant proved a moderately successful seller, and spawned a yet more potent version, the B105. Thanks to its higher compression ratio, this new model could top 90mph, and could complete the 0–60mph dash in a whisker over 12 seconds.

By this time, the Sports was beginning to show its age, and it was quietly dropped in August '59 in favour of another new model, the T60 three-wheeler. Designed to appeal to former motorcyclists, this sporting trike shared its basic design and layout with its siblings, with the exception of the single rear wheel, which was mounted centrally on a single arm, swinging from a steel crossmember moulded into the monocoque at the base of the front seats. Priced at £330, the T60 proved an instant hit, prompting the firm to introduce a four-seater variant, the T60/4, the following year.

As if that was not enough, Berkeley launched two further variations on the

Future Ferrari Grand Prix star Lorenzo Bandini en route to class honours aboard a B65 in the '59 Inter-Europe Cup, Monza.

George Catt three-wheels at Silverstone in 1960 at an AMOC meeting in his B105. A higher-compression 792cc motor was fitted to answer the demand for more power.

The B95 model featured Royal Enfield's parallel twin Constellation motor, the height of which necessitated the elevated bonnet line.

The pretty Italianate lines were not enough to secure the Bandit's future. Just two cars were made.

B90 theme. The QB95 was essentially an augmented B90, modified to produce a full four-seater (of sorts). The QB95 was only ever seen at the '59 Earls Court Motor Show and disappeared from view almost immediately. Just to confuse matters, the following year saw the revival of the Sports, now dubbed the B95.

Although Berkeley had seemingly found favour among impecunious motorists with sporting aspirations, it was soon courting disaster. The arrival of the Mini in '59 effectively spelt the end for motorcycle-based cars. The Mini was cheap, could seat four in comfort (relatively speaking), and could out-handle most sports cars. Panter ended his partnership with Bond, and put the company's future in the hands of freelance racing car designer, John Tojeiro. A decision was made to move further upmarket with a 'proper' sports car – the Bandit.

Deviating from Berkeley's standard practice of steel-reinforced glassfibre monocoque construction, the new model employed an aluminium and steel chassis, with separate glassfibre bodywork. The engine and running gear were taken from the recently introduced Ford Anglia 105E, with the race-proven Coventry Climax FWA engine proposed as a future option. Although the Bandit had a rear-wheel-drive layout, it retained the familiar rear swing-axles with combined coil springs and shock absorbers, and used a MacPherson strut front suspension layout. Inside, the Bandit was markedly more salubrious than its forebears, with a spacious cabin which could comfortably house six-footers, featuring leather-trimmed bucket seats and a comprehensively equipped dashboard. With a target price of £798 after tax, the Renault Floride-esque roadster should have been a roaring success. But it was not.

Displayed at the '60 Earls Court Motor Show, the pretty Bandit attracted more than a little interest from Ford's product development team who were embroiled in a secret sports car project of their own – which could explain why the Blue Oval refused to supply componentry, effectively killing off the project after just two prototypes had been completed.

With the caravan market in steep decline, and a bank manager tugging on the financial reins, Panter was forced to admit defeat. On December 13, 1960, the firm was placed in the hands of the receiver, and bankruptcy was declared the following month. The chairman of the creditors cited over-production in the late-'50s, and crippling development costs for the Bandit, as the reasons behind the closure. Around 4200 cars had been completed, roughly 1700 of them being T60s.

Britannia GT

The inelegant Britannia GT proved a resounding flop, entering into obscurity almost as quickly as it appeared.

The business of entrepreneurial endeavour is usually best kept at a distance from creative, well-meaning daydreamers. Charming, witty and an idealist, Acland Geddes was nothing if not determined. His many commercial ventures had crashed and burned, but his character oozed irrepressible optimism. He was in serious danger of becoming the black sheep of the family when he announced his intentions to become a motor mogul, a decision that, predictably, was to end in failure.

Geddes had long harboured dreams of building a high-performance coupé to rival Aston Martin's DB series. Geddes's dream car would have a specification so comprehensive, that there would be no need for an options list. With this outline in mind, and with the necessary finance in place, he formed Britannia Cars Ltd in December '57, with close friend Murray Beecroft. Designing cars was an alien concept to both partners, so Geddes approached two men whom he believed could help realise his vision – John Tojeiro and Cavendish Morton.

At the time, Tojeiro Automotive Developments Ltd was involved in myriad projects, including a one-off AC Le Mans racer, the company founder having already found some measure of fame in the racing world. Tojeiro's brief was to develop the AC's tubular-steel ladderframe for the new Britannia GT. Royal Academy artist Morton would then cast his highly trained eye over Beecroft's renderings of the car's fixed-head silhouette, and make any necessary styling changes.

As winter became spring, Tojeiro's Barkway workshop was a hive of activity. A rolling chassis was completed, with suspension consisting of a low, diagonal-pivot swing axle at the rear, and unequal-length wishbones plus

Britannia GT	
Made	Ashwell, Hertfordshire
Engine	Front-mounted, water-cooled 2553cc straight-six
Construction	Steel multi-tubular chassis with glassfibre body
Top speed	120mph
0–60mph	8 seconds
Price new	£2400 (1958)

Britannia Cars Ltd moved into a hastily equipped facility in Ashwell, Hertfordshire in mid-'59.

The Britannia GT was styled in part by Royal Academy artist Cavendish Morton, who refined Murray Beecroft's original design.

helical springs at the front. Hydraulic dampers were used on all four corners. Power came from a 2553cc, Ford Zephyr straight-six, with a light-alloy Raymond-Mays 12-port cylinder head, and triple SU carburettors. The engine's power was quoted as 150bhp at 5000rpm, and was transmitted to the rear 15-inch, chrome-plated, knock-off wire wheels by a modified close-ratio Jaguar 4-speed 'box. Large-diameter, servo-assisted disc brakes were fitted all-round, with the rear units mounted inboard. Steering was by rack and pinion.

The completed chassis, complete with running gear, was despatched to coachbuilder FLM (Panelcraft) Ltd of Putney, to be clothed in its new, and extremely bland, aluminium bodywork. The prototype was then returned to Barkway for completion – Geddes's brainchild had been born. Prematurely, as it transpired. During testing, the car's handling proved precarious, with masses of understeer shifting to oversteer as the rear suspension reacted nervously to camber changes and heavily rutted roads. Even so, the prototype still managed to top 125mph, and reached 60mph in a whisker over nine seconds.

As 1958 drew to a close, there was still nothing even resembling a production schedule. The project appeared to be progressing at a snail's pace, prompting a disillusioned Beecroft to resign from the company. No moulds had been produced from which production Britannia GTs could be laminated; there wasn't even a factory to build them in. News of the situation obviously reached the firm's backers as, in mid-'59, a 2000sq ft facility was found in Ashwell, Hertfordshire, and was hastily (and expensively) equipped with a fabrication shop, trimming department and painting booths. The adjoining house was converted to form offices, which Geddes lavishly furnished for himself and three office staff.

Britannia Cars Ltd now had an outward facade of professionalism; all it needed was a product to sell. If and when that product was to materialise, its specifications would read like a sports car enthusiast's wish list. According to the brochure, the GT was going to be: 'An entirely new conception in sports motoring; a combination of characteristics never before available in one car at any price.' Continuing the hyperbole, it promised: 'Limousine luxury, brilliant acceleration, superlative comfort, magnificent braking, impeccable handling and exceptional luggage space.' The list of creature comforts was indeed

The John Tojeiro-designed AC Ace Le Mans car's chassis was adapted for use on the Britannia GT.

The Britannia Formula Junior was designed by John Tojeiro and later marketed by him under his own name: a move that brought no change in fortune.

14

Just four Britannia GTs were built before Britannia Cars Ltd was placed into receivership.

impressive – leather trimming, folding rear seat, fitted luggage in the boot, and a quart tin of touch-up paint. There was even a jar of leather preservative! All this for £2400.

Geddes's somewhat overly optimistic plans called for five cars to be built per month. But as the year wore on, there were continued delays with the first production glassfibre bodies, which were made by the David Charles concern of Buntingford, Herts. Further complications were caused by an inept trainee welder, who failed to measure the stress loads on the chassis he was building. No less than 14 frames had to be scrapped because they were out of alignment.

By this time, a colossal amount of money had been sunk into the project, with nothing to show for this investment aside from a now rather dog-eared development hack. Yet Geddes still managed to persuade others to share his vision, Hong Kong Mercedes importer Walter Sulke depositing much-needed funds into the coffers in December '59. The following month, Tojeiro was made Technical Director on a part-time basis (he was also embroiled in the disastrous Berkeley Bandit project) and, in April 1960, the first glassfibre body was delivered to the Ashwell facility. But it didn't fit the chassis.

A few weeks later, a second bodyshell appeared at the factory and, after much massaging, was mated to its chassis and running gear. Geddes was by now under acute pressure from his shareholders to get production underway. The cash-flow situation was partially alleviated by an infusion of funds provided by Alfred Platts of the improbably (and ironically) named concern, Foresight Investments Ltd.

Mid-way through 1960, the first definitive GT was completed, and a second left-hand-drive example was finished a few weeks later for an American customer. But, as the production line spluttered into life, there were innumerable delays in the supply of components. Just two more cars were built before the band of increasingly irate financiers pulled the plug. Britannia Cars Ltd was placed into receivership the following December. A public auction took place in March '61, with a couple of cars selling for around £1000 each.

The usually stoic Geddes had remained buoyant throughout all the setbacks, but apparently burst into tears when the firm closed its doors for good. At one stage he had gone as far as to form a second company dubbed Britannia Developments to develop new models, but it all came to naught. John Tojeiro entertained hopes of reviving the marque with Chevrolet V8 power, and a more basic specification but, predictably, these plans foundered. He did, however, purchase parts for a Britannia Formula Junior single-seater which he had designed for the 1960 season, and built up six cars as 'Tojeiros'. Compact, with distinctive high tails, these Ford Anglia 105E-powered machines proved to be also-rans, disappearing from entry lists as swiftly as they had appeared.

Geddes's grand scheme to become a player in the motor industry was destined from the outset to be little more than a pipedream. The GT brochure trumpeted: 'The Britannia is destined to become one of the most coveted cars in the world.' In a parallel universe perhaps.

Britannia GT

The distinctive John Frayling-styled Clan Crusader was not at its happiest viewed head-on. The jutting headlights were a controversial feature.

From the jaws of victory, the Clan Crusader grabbed defeat. If there had been any justice, it would have been a roaring success. The diminutive coupé was well made, and fast, with tenacious handling, but that wasn't enough for the car to survive Britain's early-'70s political machinations. Instead, it headed for the shadows, to be appreciated by a small, adoring retinue.

It would not be stretching credulity too far to dub the Crusader a Lotus without the badge, as the brains behind the outfit were all former high-ranking employees of Colin Chapman. Marque instigator was Paul Haussauer (project engineer of the second-generation Lotus Elite) who, together with Formula 1 and Indy Car boffin Brian Luff (partially responsible for the all-conquering Lotus 72 World Championship winner), and stylist John Frayling, went it alone in '69 to produce their own sports car.

The fruit of their labours appeared in '71. The Clan Crusader positively brimmed with engineering integrity. The basis for the car was a two-piece structure – a top and a bottom effectively – bonded together, with strengthening diaphragms and localised reinforcement at key stress areas, creating a remarkably strong, yet ultra-lightweight, monocoque. Running gear came from the Sunbeam Stiletto, and the donor car's all-alloy Coventry Climax-derived ohc slant-four, swing-axle front suspension, and semi-trailing arm rear set up, were robbed virtually wholesale.

If the car's construction smacked of innovation, the styling was underwhelming. Penned by Frayling (who's CV also included the equally distinctive Lotus Europa), the Crusader was attractive in profile, if a little slab sided, but the jutting headlights were a controversial feature. If nothing else, it was different, and the Clan Motor Company wasn't lacking in orders –

Clan Crusader	
Made	Washington, County Durham
Engine	Air-cooled all-alloy 875cc 'four'
Construction	Fibreglass unitary
Top speed	99mph
0–60mph	12 seconds
Price new	£1399 (1971)

especially after *Autocar* raved about the machine in a group test with a Triumph Spitfire and a Fiat 850. The Clan was faster than its mainstream rivals (top speed around 100mph), and more economical (34.3mpg overall), but it was expensive. Offered in component form (fully trimmed, with all wiring, glass and piping in place) for £1123, or for £1339 complete, it needed to be exceptional, at a time when an MG Midget MkIII could have been yours for £930.

A steady trickle of cars crept out of temporary premises in Washington, Tyne-and-Wear, from July '71. By the time official production commenced the following September, the firm was operating out of a leased, 23,000sq ft facility in County Durham, taking advantage of a government development grant in the employment-depressed area. Before long, the trickle of cars had increased, as five cars left the factory despite a coal miners' strike that caused supply problems. This industrial action prevented, to some extent, the growth of output, and was just the start of the firm's problems.

It didn't take long for the competition fraternity to latch on to the Crusader's extraordinary dynamics. Future Nissan works-driver Andy Dawson, ably accompanied by John Foden, finished a remarkable second overall in the '72 Manx International Rally, on his car's first outing. The same season saw the Tour of Mull Rally won by Alan Conley in his Crusader, while Mike Hinde lifted the following year's Production Car Trials Championship spoils. But it wasn't just in the rough and tumble world of rallying that the Clan proved its abilities, as legendary club racer Gerry Marshall raced a works demonstrator with winning aplomb.

As 1972 dawned, there lingered the constant threat of strikes across the country. Yet, despite irregular component deliveries, Clan production was still running strongly. In May, by which time the car was no longer offered in DIY form, the Crusader was successfully crash-tested at MIRA. But, as the year wore on, the firm began to face financial problems, largely due to late

The Crusader's cabin was surprisingly comfortable, with a semi-reclined driving position.

Clan Crusader production in full swing at the firm's Washington, County Durham factory.

payment (or non payment) from creditors. And then, Chrysler, which supplied the running gear, was crippled with industrial action. With no supply of mechanical parts, there were numerous monocoques lying around awaiting finishing. As delivery dates were determined by guesswork, a number of orders were cancelled, and the Crusader's future began to look increasingly bleak.

Even so, the Clan Motor Company struggled on into '73, and even managed to scoop the prestigious Gold Medal for coachwork at the October London Motor Show, the first time that a low volume, specialist manufacturer had been awarded the prize. But it wasn't enough to save the firm. Strikes, allied to the imposition of VAT, the fuel crisis, and the three-day working week, brought the company to its knees. As Christmas loomed, the Crusader was no more: around 350 had been made. The doors were closed, and a number of incomplete cars were sold on by the receivers. But that was far from the end for the marque, the ensuing saga sullying the Clan's once highly regarded reputation.

A large proportion of Clan's assets were bought by Cypriot lorry manufacturer Andreas Kaisis, and shipped to Cyprus. However, just as Crusader manufacture was about to recommence, Turkey invaded Cyprus's northern territories. The Crusader jigs and moulds then languished under dust sheets until they were bought and rescued some years later by Briton Ian Hooper, a former colleague of Paul Haussauer.

Meanwhile, Brian Luff had begun offering his own line of Clan bodies through his Status Cars concern, having taken a mould from an original Crusader body. These 'shells were primarily sold to the competition crowd as replacements for damaged originals, although a handful were built into road cars. Luff sold around 12 bodies up until 1982, when he sold the moulds to Peter McCandless, a long-time marque devotee and the owner of an original Crusader.

Which is when the recriminations started. Haussauer was, at this time, attempting to revive the Clan, and was nonplussed when McCandless announced his intention to do likewise. A flurry of letters was exchanged but, as it transpired, Haussauer failed to get the necessary backing, so turned his

The Crusader's rear view was especially accomplished. The Clan was faster and more economical than its mainstream rivals.

back on his brainchild, and instead turned his attentions to building the virtuous but unremittingly dull Mini-based Phoenix estate car, before turning to lecturing.

McCandless, echoing the original Clan Motor Company's efforts, managed to secure a government development grant to procure a manufacturing base in Newtownards, Northern Island. Now simply known as the Clan, the car received a minor makeover, with the protruding headlights being junked in favour of pop-up units, while the bumpers were now moulded-in, with the addition of a neat chin spoiler. Most often offered as a pure kit car, requiring the customer to source components, the re-launched Clan proved a minor success. Sold in three levels – basic, deluxe and (occasionally) complete – around 120 cars were built over the ensuing four years, but McCandless was nothing if not ambitious.

The rippled rear bonnet hinged on the left for access to the Imp Sport 'four'.

In 1985, he unveiled the Clan Clover, a heavily reworked edition, with blistered arches, plus a mid-mounted, 1.5-litre Alfa Romeo flat-four 'boxer' engine. Around six of these machines were supplied in kit-form, before the switch was made to factory-built cars only. Unfortunately, the build quality and the source of the components (reputedly second-hand, rather than brand-new) prompted one disgruntled customer to voice his grievances to the media. Following a mud-slinging television 'exposé', the Clan Car Company lurched into receivership in June '87, the marque's reputation seemingly forever besmirched.

Costin

The Costin Amigo incorporated many of its designer's characteristic aerodynamic touches. The Amigo made use of Vauxhall Victor running gear.

Costin Amigo	
Made	Slaughton, Bedfordshire
Engine	Front-mounted, water-cooled 2279cc ohv 'four'
Construction	Plywood monocoque with glassfibre outer skin
Top speed	137mph
0–60mph	7.2 seconds
Price new	£3326 (1971)

By his own admission, Frank Costin was never particularly interested in cars. He viewed them as being merely a means of transport that were inefficient and poorly packaged. His background in the aircraft industry gave him a grounding in aerodynamics that he applied to myriad projects, from speedboats to spacecraft; bobsleighs to microlights. But it is for his role as champion of the black art of streamlining to the motor racing arena that he will be best remembered. He was introduced to the automotive world in the mid-'50s by younger brother Mike (the Cos of Cosworth), and penned the sleek Lotus VIII for Colin Chapman. This highly distinctive sports-racer set the trend for all future Costin-designed machines, in being innovative yet not overly attractive. The Irishman had no time for stylists or image-conscious hauteur – efficiency was paramount. Not that he was unable to produce a vision of beauty; witness the Vanwall Grand Prix car and the devilishly attractive Costin-Nathan sports-racer, but, more often than not, his creations were blindingly fast and decidedly odd in appearance.

Considering Costin's lack of passion for motoring in general, it's all the more remarkable that he should choose to go it alone and produce and manufacture his own sports car – the Costin Amigo. When he first mooted the idea in 1968, he was adamant that his dream child should be 'neither a gin palace nor a 150mph leaky trap or worse, a stylish hoax.' Costin held firm the belief that he could design a proper Gran Turismo that would appeal to enthusiasts for its performance and advanced engineering principles, rather than for any perceived status that it would convey. The basic concept called for the ability to cruise at 100mph at less than 5000rpm, while offering comfort and civility. The car would be capable of high performance, but in

Frank Costin at the wheel of an incomplete Costin-Nathan sports-racer, the progenitor of the Costin Amigo.

safety, with features such as deformable boxed sections, a roll-over bar and a breakaway fuel cell.

The Amigo's basis was a timber monocoque, with three long box-sections running longitudinally, one forming the centre transmission tunnel, the others extending from the front to the rear wheel wells. Strips of Parana pine were bonded to the structure for reinforcement and, as in Costin's previous wooden-hulled racing cars, a synthetic-resin glue, Aerolite, was the only bonding agent. The frame featured built-in seats, made of curved sheets of plywood with an inch of foam rubber between the wood and upholstery,

The GT version of the Costin-Nathan sports-racer was a stunningly attractive design.

From head on, the Amigo appeared woefully ill-proportioned. Many of Frank Costin's characteristic aerodynamic touches can be seen here.

based on a development of Costin's orthopaedic chair. Typical of his attention to detail, the chassis featured such novelties as a hatch in the lower rear body section to house the spare wheel, and a wooden chamber home for the alloy fuel tank that would eject on impact, both of which were positioned low in the frame to offset the driver's weight. The bare chassis with suspension subframes tipped the scales at a mere 187lbs.

Despite the advanced, if unusual, methods of construction, Costin's choice of the deathly dull Vauxhall Victor as a source for the Amigo's running gear was anything other than exotic. But, typically, there was sound logic behind his reasoning. The Amigo was to be reliable and easy to work on, and the Victor's 2-litre OHC 'four' was just about unburstable. The engine was mounted directly on the chassis via heavily armoured brackets, with the Victor's pressed-steel front crossmember acting as the subframe locating the upper and lower wishbones. The rear suspension used the Vauxhall's axle, located by parallel leading links and a Panhard rod. Koni self-levelling hydro-pneumatic dampers were fitted all-round.

Unusually for Costin, the Amigo's body was made of glassfibre (although the prototype was alloy-skinned), incorporating many of his characteristic aerodynamic touches, such as exterior hinges hidden within low-drag fairings that also included a cockpit air-intake feeding eyeball-vents on the dashboard. Another oddity was the 'visual warning indicator', consisting of a roof-mounted pylon, with a fixed flashing light at its top, to enable other road users to see the low-slung GT over hedge rows, while also cunningly concealing the radio aerial.

Three years elapsed before the Amigo was ready for public consumption, during which time Costin had taken on backers to keep the project afloat. Jack Wiggins was a television executive and sports car enthusiast who'd paid a substantial deposit for the first car but, shortly after he handed over the cash, another potential saviour entered the scene. Paul Pyecroft had met with minor success in club racing behind the wheel of various Jaguars, and formed an alliance with Costin, convincing him to pitch the Amigo further upmarket; a move that left Wiggins out in the cold without a car – much to Costin's continued regret – and caused conflict between the two partners that would ultimately play a part in the Amigo's demise.

The decision to substantially raise the price of the car to £3300 put the Amigo in select company in 1971. It was out of reach to most enthusiasts and in the clutches of desirable Italian hardware. Journalists were swift to praise the car's dynamics, and commended its performance and poise, although they were rather less enamoured by its fixed Perspex side screens, small, difficult to negotiate doors, and stark cabin, which were unbecoming of such an expensive machine. And then there was the styling, that might not have mattered all that much to Costin, but met with resounding condemnation from most onlookers. A riot of bulges and odd proportions, it could never be considered remotely attractive. In short, the Amigo was a case of substance over style and, while it met with Costin's stringent criteria (it could top 137mph with a standard engine, returning 30mpg at a constant 60mph), it failed to tug on the public's heart (and purse) strings.

In a bid to broaden its appeal by picking up some competition kudos, an attempt was made on the '71 six-hour enduro at Le Mans. A car was prepared with a Brian Hart-tuned 1599cc Ford twin-cam, and ultra-lightweight body, and on paper it looked to have its class opposition on the ropes. Most of the wheels from a batch that was specially made for this foray were supplied with the wrong offset, but, since punctures were so rare, the decision was made to crack on with just the one set of rims. Hart, who some years earlier had driven Costin's Protos Formula 2 car, held an eight-mile class lead after the first hour, recording a top speed of 147mph along the Mulsanne Straight, then a tyre picked up some debris and burst, damaging the wheel. Undaunted, an attack on the following year's 24-hour race at La Sarthe was mooted once full-scale production had commenced.

It never did, as the relationship between Costin and Pyecroft soon soured. By 1972, seven cars had left the former's tiny Welsh workshop and, though a new, much larger facility had been found at Little Staughton Airfield in Bedfordshire, the once-envisaged run of 120 cars per year failed to materialise after Pyecroft relinquished the company to Costin. Further backing was sought, but none was found, and Costin Automotive Racing Products went into voluntary liquidation. Enquiries from would-be entrepreneurs keen to take on the project as a whole entity fell on deaf ears, as Costin was unwilling to allow the Amigo to be revived by anyone of less exacting standards than himself.

The rear three-quarter view of the Amigo showed Kamm-tail and 'flying buttresses'.

Deep Sanderson

The Martin V8-engined Deep Sanderson 303 in action. This car competed in the '69 Nürburgring 1000 kilometres, surviving for six hours of the race.

The maxim 'If at first you don't succeed, try, try again' could have been coined especially for Chris Lawrence. In a forty-year career, he has created myriad automotive designs, encompassing everything from seismic supercars to faux vintage Bentley roadsters; diminutive GTs to luxury saloons, many of them bearing the bizarre Deep Sanderson moniker. Some of his creations have reached almost iconic status, while others have swiftly disappeared into the ether to languish in obscurity. Always a maverick, Lawrence has never been fettered by engineering constraints, revelling in his freedom of expression.

But it is as a Morgan racer and tuner that Lawrence initially found fame. After dabbling with hillclimbing in the mid-'50s, using a Jap-powered trike while an impecunious engineering student, he made his circuit debut aboard a German AFM, powered by a de-stroked BMW 328 engine. This car was quickly superseded by a Microplas-bodied special based on one of the famed Three Musketeers MG NE Magnette trials cars. Having earned his stripes in club racing, and with an eye to becoming a professional racing driver, the young Lawrence then purchased a three-year-old Morgan Plus 4, registered TOK 258, and proceeded to win the '58 Freddie Dixon trophy series with the self-prepared Triumph-engined roadster. Such was his dominance, that he was persuaded to prepare similar cars for rivals, forming Lawrencetune, with friends Leslie Fagg and Len Bridge, the following year.

Buoyed by success in domestic races, Lawrence turned his attention to international competition, with a Lola Mk1 and his faithful and increasingly powerful Morgan, the highlight being a class-win and thirteenth overall in the '62 Le Mans 24-hour classic, sharing TOK 258 with Richard Shepherd-Barron. It was the beginning of a love affair with the French enduro, the young

Deep Sanderson 301	
Made	Acton, London
Engine	Mid-mounted, water-cooled 1275cc ohv 'four'
Construction	Tubular spaceframe with glassfibre body
Top speed	110mph
0–60mph	10 seconds
Price new	N/A (built to order)

The original Deep Sanderson 301 unveiled at the '62 Racing Car Show earned the nickname 'perfume delivery wagon'.

The ludicrously quick DS 501 'Twini' blasts off the line at Blackbushe at the Sydney Allard Dragfest in '63.

engineer having already decided to return the following year with a car of his own design.

Lawrence had built a Ford pre-crossflow-powered Formula Junior single-seater in 1960, dubbed the Deep Sanderson, but this ungainly device proved unsuccessful and the project was soon dropped. As was the unhappy-looking Triumph Herald-based DS201 sports car of the same year, which remained unique. With lessons learned from these lamentable episodes, his next foray into automotive design proved more successful, if no more attractive.

The decidedly odd-looking Deep Sanderson 301 was unleashed on an unsuspecting public at the '61 Racing Car Show. Power came from a rear, transversely-mounted Mini A-series engine, fitted to a backbone chassis, the unique Lawrence-link trailing-arm suspension set-up being used all-round. This system, according to the designer, gave no track variation and complete camber compensation. Clothing the frame was a bizarre, ill-proportioned alloy body, with a long, bulbous nose and 'bread van' tail. These features swiftly earned the car the moniker of 'perfume delivery wagon' after it featured in a Brockbank cartoon.

Lawrence raced and sprinted the prototype with some success, before an accident in the closing stages of the '61 Nürburgring 1000 kilometres, while lying third in the up-to-1000cc class. The crumpled wreck returned to his Acton, West London workshop, and remained there for 12 months as other projects took precedence, before Williams & Pritchard were commissioned to build a new coupé body in time for the January '63 Racing Car Show. Sitting just 36 inches tall, the revised 301 broke with Deep Sanderson tradition in being pretty. Production cars were sold in kit form with glassfibre bodies.

Contemporary road tests were highly complementary but, from the outset, the 301 was intended as a competition tool, Lawrence's equipe returning to La Sarthe in '63. An excursion into the sand banks three laps into the race cost the team dearly, but amazingly, by half distance the Deep Sanderson was leading its class, only to be withdrawn for a technical infringement. Undaunted, Lawrence returned in '64, with two cars, for what was to prove

The restyled 301 was infinitely more attractive than the original. This view shows the excellent engine access.

a disastrous weekend. His own 1275cc example was comfortably leading its class early in the race, having been clocked at 146mph down the Mulsanne Straight, only to retire after four hours with oil pump trouble. The sister car, driven by Jim Donnelly, and powered by a 1360cc Downton-tuned A-series, was faster still, but was written off in practice. Then, on the return drive to the UK, Lawrence crashed his Chevrolet Corvair, prompting a lengthy stay in hospital and, consequently, the end of 301 production after just 14 cars had been completed.

After recuperating, Lawrence campaigned his wacky twin-Downton A-series-engined DS 501 'Twini' single-seater in Formula Libre events, before becoming embroiled in the ill-starred Pearce-Ferrari Grand Prix project. Lawrence sporadically drove this F1 single-seater during the '66 season, the highlight being a fifth place in the Oulton Park Gold Cup, before a mysterious fire in the paddock put paid to the team. Lawrence shifted his attentions to tuning Vauxhalls, and myriad non car-related projects, before attempting another Le Mans attack. In late-'67, the class-leading 301 from the '64 running of the 24-hour race was exhumed and modified out of all recognition. The wheelbase was extended by nine inches, and the chassis reworked to accept a 1650cc Ford pushrod engine, with Telecalemit-Jackson fuel-injection, and a Hewland 'box. The rear suspension was now a de Dion arrangement with transverse wishbones, and the front end of the car was suspended by wishbones and coil springs. Now christened the 302, the car proved unwieldy in testing, but was fully sorted in time for the '68 Le Mans 24 Hours, with Lawrence sharing driving duties with John

The gorgeous Chris Spender-styled SLR coupé. Just four were made; three with Morgan chassis, and one with Triumph TR4 running gear.

Wingfield. Again, the Deep Sanderson was the fastest car in its class, but it retired after three hours after the fuel-injection pump drive broke.

His enthusiasm undimmed, Lawrence plotted another attempt on the following year's race at Le Mans, the hard-worked 302 now reworked to accept a 3-litre Martin V8 motor. Redesignated the 303, it was denied an entry at La Sarthe, but did compete in the Nürburgring 1000 kilometres where, after two accidents during practice, it survived six hours of the race. Lawrencetune development engineer Peter Dodds, who had campaigned the car in club meetings with some success, subsequently bought the 303.

By this time, motor sport increasingly took a back seat, as Lawrence and his team became entangled in the tortuous Monica project. Industrialist Jean Tastevin dreamed of building a grand routier in the tradition of the Facel Vega, and initially approached the Englishman with an order for tuned straight-six engines, but Lawrence managed to persuade Tastevin to let him design and engineer the entire car. The first aluminium-bodied prototype was completed in late-'67 with Triumph power, and sported a Deep Sanderson badge. A Martin

The Deep Sanderson 302 was reworked to accept the impressive Martin 3-litre V8 motor, and redesignated the 303.

Deep Sanderson

The ill-starred Vignale-styled Monica pictured in Lyon with a development mule behind. The move to steel body construction resulted in the car being 550lbs overweight.

V8 was mooted for production cars, but manufacturer Coventry Victor lurched into receivership after just 14 units had been completed.

Meanwhile, Italian *carrozzeria* Vignale was commissioned to give the car a styling makeover, Lawrence's own effort being distinctive if not overly appealing. Unfortunately, the move to steel body construction resulted in the now renamed Monica (after Tastevin's wife) being 550lb overweight. Plans to subcontract Jensen Motors to build the car came to naught, so a production line was set up in France. As of '72, a lightly modified 5.6-litre Chrysler V8 became standard equipment, which endowed the portly saloon with brisk but not stupefying performance. By late-'74, the newly renamed Monica 560 was finally ready for production but, sadly, in those fuel-conscious days, it lasted only a few months

Barely seven production cars were completed, along with 25 prototypes. Lawrence sold the final batch of four cars to Brabham Grand Prix boss Bernie Ecclestone (for a song, apparently), and the tooling and manufacturing rights passed to Robert Jankel's Panther Westwinds concern, although plans to reintroduce the car came to naught. Tastevin's dream of building 'La Jaguar Francais' had turned into a nightmare.

After the project collapsed, Lawrence drifted away from cars for several years, developing winches for racing yachts, before moving to America, where he set up shop preparing historic racing cars. He has now returned from his self-imposed exile, and is currently engaged in designing a new breed of hi-tech Morgan. He is also threatening to reintroduce the Deep Sanderson 301.

Deep Sanderson

Diva

An original Diva coupé betrays its Heron Europa-derived bodyshell. The car was originally intended as a one-off.

For all its success in '60s sports car racing, the Diva marque presently lingers in a netherworld between obscurity and hazy recognition. The name might sound vaguely familiar but, to even the most enlightened enthusiasts, Diva remains a dim and fitful memory. But then the man behind the name never did court publicity, preferring to let the results do the talking. Which they did – briefly.

Back in the mid-'50s, Don Sim was a partner with Mike Handley in Yimkin Engineering, specialising in tuning BMC A- and B-series engines. In 1958, the firm unveiled a stark 'clubmans' sports car in the Lotus Seven idiom. A tidy and efficient design, there was nothing especially radical to its make up: spaceframe chassis, double-wishbone front suspension, and a skimpy alloy body to keep at least some of the rain off. Around six of these cycle-winged sportsters were made, quickly racking up race results, and prompting a small run of glassfibre-bodied Formula Junior single-seaters. But the London firm folded in 1960, as the principals got married and pursued different interests.

In 1961, Sim formed Tunex Conversions in Camberwell, South-East London. But the lure of building cars was never far away. He was keen to raise the firm's profile as an engine tuner, and the following year saw the arrival of the Diva coupé. Intended from the outset as a one-off, the car's basis was a compact spaceframe, with all-round independent suspension, front disc brakes, and a 997cc Tunex-Ford four-pot. Rather than going to the trouble of producing his own body for the frame, Sim commissioned Heron Plastics of Greenwich to come up with a bespoke 'shell. Instead, Heron modified one of its pretty 750-special units, and used the same style of 'shell for its Heron

Diva GT	
Made	West London
Engine	Front-mounted, water-cooled 997cc ohv 'four'
Construction	Tubular spaceframe with glassfibre body
Top speed	115mph
0–60mph	9 seconds
Price new	N/A (built to order)

Europa coupé. This also explains the Diva's dead-ringer likeness to the Europa-based MBM offered by Switzerland's Peter Monteverdi.

An attractive, if slightly effete, coupé, the race-inspired one-off generated a great deal of interest from hot shoes throughout England's club racing scene. Doug Bloomfield drove the prototype in a number of meetings during the '62 season, the car proving blisteringly fast, but fragile. Although the original intention was to promote Tunex, punters seemed more interested in the car than the modded engines. So the Diva made it into production and, towards the end of the year, a second car was built by Heron, with a larger windscreen offering better frontal vision. Over Christmas, a further five

Future Formula One driver John Miles (151) and Doug Bloomfield (150) give chase to the Braysan Diva in their similar examples.

cars were made, dubbed Diva B-types. These cars were offered with a range of Ford 'fours', Doug Mockford's example proving the class of the field throughout '63.

Though the car was offered for street use, the entire Diva production run went to the racing fraternity. The design was further refined in '63, with a choice of 1340cc or 1650cc Ford engines. Around 13 of these diminutive coupés were sold over the following 18 months, the Diva proving the car to beat in national GT events, also scooping class honours in the '64 Nürburgring 1000 Kilometres enduro. But Sim remained keen to attract custom from punters looking for performance road cars. The D-type, which was introduced in '65, featured a longer, reprofiled nose, a fully decked-out cabin, and rubber engine mountings to reduce noise. But, much to Sim's chagrin, nobody took the car seriously as an alternative to a Lotus Elan or a TVR Grantura.

Undeterred, he pressed on with another road car project, the '65 London Racing Car Show seeing the debut of Diva's first mid-engined sports car, the Demon. Looking uncannily like a Porsche 904 that had been left under a hot light, this oddly proportioned machine featured the expected spaceframe chassis, with Hillman Imp power. The Rootes Group gave its blessing to the project, agreeing to supply running gear, and even expressed an interest in taking over the production rights. However, once again, all enquiries came from the competition crowd. Rootes's interest soon waned, causing Sim to change tack, junking Imp power in place of 1.5-litre Ford and 2.7-litre Coventry Climax FPF engines. The car was renamed the Valkyr, and the suspension was comprehensively reworked for the rigours of racing, while the wing-line received a flared lip to house wider wheel rims. Six Valkyrs were subsequently made over the next three years, two of them being exported.

Sim's parting shot at persuading sceptical sports car buyers that his products could be used on the road was the 10F of '66. This latest variant was marketed as a non-competition model, not that anybody noticed.

Doug Bloomfield wards off a determined Peter Davis (Ginetta G4) aboard his Diva D-type.

Diva

Despite a more substantial, thicker glassfibre body, and extensive sound deadening, all of the three examples made were to spend their time flogging around racetracks. The 10F's smoother body style was, however, subsequently used on D-types.

In early '67, Sim sold out to Enfield Automotive, the Isle-of-Wight-based purveyors of unappealing electric cars and equally repellent luxury off-roaders. 'Sleeping partner' John de Bruyn meanwhile left to pursue his ultimately futile Gordon-Keeble revival scheme. Divas were technically offered for another twelve months, but it remains doubtful that any more were actually made. Around 66 coupés of all types had been built. All were road-registered but, without exception, the entire production run was used purely for trackside outings. Press releases were later issued for a gas-turbine Le Mans car, showing a picture of a Valkyr. Despite news items in the motor sport glossies, nothing more was ever heard of this intriguing project.

Though Sim failed utterly in educating the public as to the virtues of Diva road cars, the marque left behind a remarkable run of racing results: around 200 in total, including a further success in the Nürburgring 1000 Kilometres, taking class honours in the '68 running. Divas also finished first and second in the up-to-1150cc category of the Wills International Trophy, and lifted the hard-fought '67 Redex spoils. These barely recognised coupés also paved the way to Formula 1 for John Miles and Jackie Oliver, two of the most successful Diva protagonists. A remarkable pedigree for a marque seemingly forever consigned to darkness in enthusiasts' memory banks.

Though conceived primarily as a road car, the Diva Valkyr found greater success as a racer. A total of six were built.

Diva

Elva

The Elva GT160 proved the undoubted showstopper at the '64 Geneva Salon, and was universally praised by the motoring press.

Elva Courier T-type	
Made	Croydon, Surrey
Engine	Front-mounted, water-cooled 1798cc ohv 'four'
Construction	Ladderframe chassis with glassfibre body
Top speed	110mph
0–60mph	9 seconds
Price new	£827 (1964)

Like so many stories from within the specialist sports car chronicles, the Elva saga began with an enthusiast who wanted to go racing. In the early-'50s, Frank Nichols owned a modest but successful garage in Bexhill. In nearby Hastings, a budding designer, Mike Chapman, had just put the finishing touches to his CSM sports-racer, powered by a Ford 10 sidevalve 'four', and constructed around a multi-tubular chassis. This skimpy device could top 100mph, but Nichols believed he could eke-out more power from the asthmatic 1172cc engine and, together with his mechanic, devised an overhead inlet valve conversion. Such was the boost in power (around 60 per cent), that it wasn't long before other wannabe motor sport heroes asked Nichols to prepare their engines.

Nichols began offering the conversion as a kit, deciding that he and his team should devise another car that would act as a useful advertisement for the tuning business. In early '55, the rolling chassis was completed, with a simplistic aluminium skin. But such was this special's success in club racing, that Nichols was inundated with requests for replicas. Thus, the Elva marque was born, the name coming from a contraction of Elle va – French for 'She goes.'

Soon, Elva Engineering was producing cars, quoting a delivery time of around four to six weeks. The bare frame cost £120, the complete kit £350. News of the firm's achievements reached Chuck Dietrich in America, resulting in an order for the first of many Elvas to go Stateside. Walter Dickson of Continental Motors was also impressed, and was appointed as the firm's US importer. Dickson persuaded Nichols that the firm's future lay in manufacturing road cars. With Dickson guaranteeing that he would buy the first year's production, the Courier was born in '58.

Designed by Peter Nott and Tim Fry (one of the prime movers behind the Hillman Imp), the Courier featured a tubular ladder-frame chassis, with 1489cc MGA power. Front suspension was independent, the Riley 1.5 rear beam axle located by radius arms and a Panhard rod. The engine sat far back in the chassis, giving a near perfect 50/50 weight distribution, cockpit ergonomics being an unfortunate casualty. Although the prototype was clothed in aluminium, production cars sported glassfibre 'shells.

From a new purpose-built factory in Bexhill-on-Sea, a steady trickle of Couriers emerged, a large proportion heading for the 'States, where they proved giant slayers in SCCA racing – among early pilots was Mark Donahue, who would later go on to conquer the Indianapolis 500 and the Can-Am championship. But the diminutive Elva was a crude machine, and in early '61 Nichols produced the Series 2 to address many of the criticisms levelled at the car. The most obvious visual change was a curved, single pane windscreen, and a revised dashboard layout. More important developments occurred underneath, with a new backbone chassis incorporating spaceframe attachments. Announced at the 1961 London Racing Car Show, this latest variant came complete with an enlarged 1588cc MG motor, and the additional option of a hardtop.

A few months earlier, Elva had also unveiled a fixed-head edition, with a distinctive (or ugly for the less charitable) Ford Anglia 105E-esque raked-back rear window. This model also featured all-round independent suspension, and front disc brakes. Production of all models was now running at the rate of around nine cars a week, but disaster was looming around the corner. Dickson failed to pay for a shipment of Couriers, having run into financial problems. That he went on to serve gaol time was of little consolation to Nichols, who was forced to liquidate his company.

Salvation appeared in the unlikely form of Trojan Ltd, famed before World

Elva's early efforts were generally sold as bare chassis for the fitment of proprietary bodyshells, such as the Falcon Shells affair seen here.

Elva

War II for its stark economy cars, and now acting as Lambretta's UK arm. The Croydon concern bought the rights to the Courier, and Nichols meanwhile pursued his first love – building purpose-built racing cars – with the backing of US racing car importer Carl Haas.

Courier production resumed in September '62, in further-revised Series III form. The engine was moved further forward to free up more cabin space, which had a detrimental effect on handling, causing terminal understeer. Nichols was brought in to rectify the problem – he simply returned the engine back to its original position. The firm also introduced a new variation on the theme, the MkIV coupé, which had a streamlined rear body section with room for two children in the back. However, the styling wasn't altogether happy looking, and didn't enter production until the following year, only to be dropped not long after.

Rather more successful was the MkIV T-type Courier, which was unveiled at the '63 Earls Court Motor Show. Identifiable by its new, smoother front and rear bodywork, this latest variant boasted a modified and strengthened box-section chassis, with 'Tru-Track' all-round independent suspension. Discernibly more civilised than its forebear, the T-type featured such niceties as wind-up windows, and an occasional rear bench seat. Engine options included the 1.8-litre MG B-series unit, and the 1558cc Ford Cortina GT 'four'. With the former in place, the MkIV could reach 60mph in eight seconds. Elva claimed that it was the only open two-seater sports car with independent suspension that was available in the UK for less than £1000.

But Trojan's back-room boffins weren't finished. To cash in on the Courier's achievements in American endurance racing, Elva unveiled the Sebring edition at the '64 London Racing Car Show. This stripped-down model sported a lightweight frame and a body made from thinner-than-standard glassfibre, with heavily tuned Lotus twin-cam power, a limited-slip differential, and magnesium wheels. However, it failed to excite the punters, and just four were made. A further, more extreme take on the theme, with Chevrolet V8 power and an Arthur Rosthan-penned GT body, failed to make it off the drawing board.

By this time, Trojan's interest in the Courier was on the wane, due to it being increasingly engrossed in Frank Nichols's racing endeavours and Bruce McLaren's embryonic racing team, eventually taking over the New Zealander's customer car operation, leaving McLaren to concentrate on his works cars. Production rights to the Courier passed to Ken Sheppard's Customised Sports Cars concern in Shenley, Hertfordshire. Not that Trojan or Frank Nichols had lost interest in the road car market.

The first, alloy-bodied Courier prototype. Production cars were fitted with glassfibre 'shells.

Near-ready Couriers waiting for final detailing at Elva's Croydon premises in 1962.

The MkIV T-type Courier was identifiable by its smoother front and rear bodywork.

The ungainly Courier MkIV coupé at the Earls Court Motor Show.

Through his various racing projects, Nichols had established friendly relations with Alex von Falkenhausen of BMW, who agreed to supply powerplants for a new mid-engined sports car. Derived from Elva's Mk VII-S sports-racer, this new machine signalled the firm's intention to move the marque further up-market. Nichols wanted Ogle to style the car, and had made an approach to director Sir John Whitmore, but Peter Agg, Trojan's managing director, was adamant that in order to gain credibility, the new and, as yet, unnamed machine should be penned by an Italian. So three chassis were dispatched to Carrozzeria Fissore in Turin, to be styled by Paris-domiciled Trevor Fiore.

When unveiled at the '64 Geneva Salon, the Elva GT160 proved the undoubted showstopper. Sitting just 40 inches off the deck, and 12ft 6in long, the low-slung coupé had a purity of line that was truly timeless. *Style Auto* dedicated seven pages to the newcomer, waxing lyrical about the 'Cartesian represented by the geometric grafting of curvilinear moduli into a single form' (answers on a postcard), so the design world was shocked to learn that Trevor Fiore was in fact Englishman, Trevor Frost. Believing that he would never be taken seriously as a stylist with such a humble name, he concealed his identity. It worked – he would go on to become head of

35

Ken Sheppard aboard a Trojan-built Courier in October '65. Sheppard's Customised Sports Cars concern took over the Courier production rights from Trojan.

Citroën's design department after penning the Trident, Alpine A310 (depending on who you ask), and Renault 25.

With its 2-litre BMW power mated to a Hewland five-speed 'box, the GT160 was universally praised by the motoring press but, sadly, it was never to make it into series production. Legend has it that when building the prototypes, pounds were confused with kilograms, resulting in excessive weight. The truth, however, is that the Latin coachbuilder had a problem with pounds sterling – production bodies were going to cost considerably more than first envisaged. Nichols was keen to market the GT160 for around £2700, which put it in elite company. Any higher, and it would be priced out of the market. So all thoughts of producing 40 cars per year went out of the window. Deposits were returned, and the GT160 was dead.

The three prototypes languished under dust sheets in a corner of Trojan's Croydon works until the Honourable Richard Wrottesley, 22-year-old heir to Lord Wrottesley, formed Anglian Racing with friend Bill Beedie, purchasing chassis number one for an attack on the '65 Le Mans classic. The car was repainted in Chinese Peacock – or metallescent purple – and appeared at La Sarthe for the April practice weekend, where the tuned 193bhp engine pulled strongly, if a little too strongly for the fragile gearbox, which repeatedly broke.

After an aborted attempt at the Targa Florio road race, next up was

Only four examples of the Lotus-powered Courier Sebring were made.

A dapper Frank Nichols poses next to the Fiore-styled GT160. Only three examples of this model were built.

ELVA-BMW 2-LITRE GT '160'

Setting a new trend in 2 litre motoring, the Elva BMW GT 160S is a most noteworthy marriage of ultra high speed performance with advanced body styling. Only 40 elegant inches high this aluminium bodied, closed two-seater coupe introduces the exciting 'low look'—the result of collaboration by the masters, Fiore of Paris and Fissore of Savigliano Italy. Whether on the competition circuit which inspired its birth, or gliding on its grand touring way, the Elva represents a breakthrough in championship quality . . . assuring for it a place in motoring hearts that only the most coveted cars can attain.

Richard Wrottesley in his GT160 shortly before being black-flagged at Mallory Park in September '65.

the Nürburgring 1000 Kilometres, where Wrottesley managed to lose the rear bodywork somewhere around the seventeen-and-a-half-mile circuit during the warm up. During the race, a drive-shaft broke after three laps, prompting instant retirement before co-driver Tony Lanfranchi took over for his stint. For the June Le Mans race, fixed headlamps replaced the pop-up units and, despite numerous transmission problems, the GT160 recorded 165mph along the Mulsanne Straight. The car proved competitive early on, but its gearbox gave up the ghost after four hours, and that was the end of Wrottesley's Elva adventure.

Trojan meanwhile toyed with the idea of producing the GT160 with a glassfibre body, but these plans ultimately came to nothing, as the firm became increasingly disinterested in Elva, pushing ahead with its own eponymous racing cars. All three GT160s then passed to Ken Shepherd, who had been producing Couriers virtually single-handedly. Shepherd installed an all-alloy, overbored 3.6-litre Buick V8 in one, but his attempts to manufacture the car himself were hindered by lack of funds. Shepherd, too, gradually lost interest in producing cars, calling it quits in '68.

One last-gasp effort at an Elva revival was initiated by marque expert Tony Ellis, who unleashed the 3000 coupé that same year. Penned by Ellis himself, it bore a distinct resemblance to previous Couriers, but underneath it was a very different proposition. The prototype featured a tubular spaceframe, with all-round independent suspension, and a 144bhp, 3-litre Ford V6. Capable of 138mph, and 0–60mph in 6.5 seconds, it received rave reviews from motoring hacks, *Hot Car* stating: 'Coupled with shattering acceleration is road holding that has to be experienced to be believed. It is literally like driving a well-balanced racing car on the road.'

In spite of all the positive hype, the 3000 (also known as the Cougar) never made it into production. Ellis had high hopes of building up to six cars per week but, without the necessary funding, the project was quietly dropped. With it died the Elva marque, more's the pity.

Elva

Fairthorpe

Torix Bennett's Fairthorpe
TXS was not the sales
success it should have been,
despite admirable build
quality and technical
innovation.

Fairthorpe Electron Minor MkIII	
Made	Gerrards Cross, Buckinghamshire
Engine	Front-mounted, water-cooled 1147cc ohv 'four'
Construction	Ladderframe chassis with glassfibre body
Top speed	87mph
0–60mph	17 seconds
Price new	£895 (1963)

In aviation circles, the late Air Vice-Marshall Don 'Pathfinder' Bennett's name is still uttered with reverential tones. War hero and record holder, he literally wrote the book on air navigation, but his second career as a car manufacturer wasn't to prove quite so illustrious. In peacetime, industry was being urged to 'export or die', and consequently new cars were in short supply. Bennett hit upon the idea of building a small, basic 'people's car', and the resultant Fairthorpe Atom was unleashed on an unsuspecting public in 1953. It boasted an impressive specification – all-round independent suspension, and rear-mounted BSA power – but its faintly comical appearance, and impossibly crude construction, meant it was always going to be doomed to failure. Moving the engine to the front of the car brought no change in fortune, and neither did convertible and panel-van derivatives.

Bennett swiftly changed tack, with the first of many sporting Fairthorpes, the Electron, emerging in late-1956. This pretty roadster wasn't the last word in sophistication, and cost more than a Triumph TR2, but it soon proved reasonably popular with the racing fraternity. Initially using a rakish Microplas bodyshell, the Electron was offered with Triumph running gear, and the option of either 1.1 to 1.5-litre Coventry Climax engines, or alternatively the ill-fated, air-cooled Butterworth flat four. Keen to reach a wider audience, Fairthorpe exhibited a revised version at the '57 Earls Court Motor Show. An in-house restyle, the new look included a fresh bonnet, and ungainly fins grafted on to the tail. This makeover was, if anything, a retrograde step, and looked a touch amateurish compared to many of the cheaper 'specials' on offer at the time.

But the marque came of age in 1956, with the highly capable, if not hugely

The comical Fairthorpe Atom found few takers. This crude contraption used rear-mounted BSA power.

John Green was a regular victor in speed events with this Standard-powered Electron Minor. Here he is seen at the '58 Westbrooke Hillclimb.

attractive, Electron Minor. Designed by John Green (who would later pen the hugely successful Daren sports-racing cars), this new model used Standard 10 running gear and, despite having only 38bhp on tap, proved a sprightly performer (although factory figures exceeding 90mph were, at best, fanciful). Offered in component-form from 1958, the Electron Minor undercut its mainstream rivals by a considerable percentage. However, by the end of the year, BMC had introduced the Austin-Healey Sprite, which was identically priced, and infinitely better made. Fairthorpe responded with the revised MkII in 1960, powered by a choice of Standard-Triumph and Ford four-cylinder motors, the biggest development being a new independent rear suspension set-up in place of the previous beam-axle arrangement.

The same year saw the Fairthorpe line-up augmented by the arrival of two new models. Although visually similar to the Electron Minor, the fearsome Zeta was almost six inches longer, with a more substantial twin-rail chassis. Triumph's TR3 provided the front and rear suspension, with power coming from a Ford Zephyr straight-six, equipped with a BRM cylinder head, and six Amal carburettors, which enabled a 0–60mph time of around 7.5 seconds.

Unfortunately, while the Zeta was undoubtedly fast, it only served to heighten Fairthorpe's unfortunate reputation for poor styling and dire build quality, *Sporting Motorist* finding: 'Where sheer performance per pound is considered, there are few cars that can excel it … The less said about the standard of finish, both internally and externally, the better.' Just five examples were made, one of them with TR2 power. Its even lumpier sibling, the Electrina

Marque founder Don Bennett threads his Electron Minor through the Gorge de la Clue on the '59 Monte Carlo rally.

saloon, fared little better. Essentially an Electron Minor with a fixed lid, the lofty roof line (moulded off a MkI Jaguar), misshapen wheel arches, and squared-off doors, conspired to produce an outline that was particularly unattractive. Priced at £498 with the choice of Standard-Triumph or Ford engines, it found just six takers.

A further variation on the Electron Minor theme arrived in late-1962, the Rockette being four inches longer than its predecessor in order to house the newly announced 1596cc Triumph Vitesse straight-six. The Electron Minor was a fine performer, and *The Autocar* found that: 'It could be hurled into corners with considerable satisfaction and virtually no qualms.' However, the addition of a third headlight, which was grafted into the middle of the nose,

gave it a bizarre appearance. Intended as an additional aid for rallying, only three customers opted for this arrangement, and a more conventional bonnet was swiftly substituted.

Meanwhile, development of the enduring Electron Minor continued apace, and the MkIII edition was unveiled at the October '63 Earls Court Motor Show. The wheelbase had been lengthened to seven feet, the raised bonnet line and new windscreen (rear glass from a Morris Oxford) providing a more cohesive silhouette. Under the bonnet remained the 1147cc Triumph 'four', with the option of various Ford units. The MkIV edition followed not long after, with revised suspension settings, but production soon dwindled to nothing. By 1970, when the MkV was unveiled with a longer tail section, the Electron Minor was absurdly archaic. A final evolution, the MkVI, was effectively an Electron Minor body mounted on a Triumph GT6 chassis, but just two were made in 1970.

By this time, Don Bennett was engrossed in myriad other projects, his son, Torix, having taken over the reins. A gifted engineer, Torix's introduction to the family firm had begun much earlier. He had acted as co-driver for his father on the '62 Monte Carlo rally, before building his own special, christened Bluebelle, around the remains of an Atom. Torix believed that Fairthorpe's

Robert Linwood's rare Zeta forms part of the winning relay team at an AMOC event at Silverstone, 1960.

future lay in producing more upmarket machines, and his first major solo effort was the TX1, which was displayed at the '65 Earls Court Motor Show. Essentially a test bed for his ingenious suspension design, it was a markedly more forward-thinking design than his father's previous efforts. Underneath its slab-sided silhouette, lay a modified Electron Minor frame, with a 1499cc Ford Cortina GT engine and 'box, plus a trailing-link and transverse-rod rear suspension set-up.

Though the car was never actively promoted, Torix Bennett had hoped that the TX1 would attract the major motor manufacturers towards his suspension ideas, as he had patented his design under the Fairthorpe Technical Exponents banner. No interest was forthcoming but, undeterred, he pushed ahead the following year with a coupé variant – the TX GT, this time using 2-litre Triumph straight-six power.

No Fairthorpe can ever be accused of being attractive, but this new model was better styled than most, although the roofline was to some extent dictated by the use of a Triumph GT6 tailgate. Underneath, the TX GT retained the TX1's intriguing rear suspension set-up fitted to a modified GT6 chassis. Offered in kit-form (£954), or turn-key (£1361), it failed to ignite the expected spark of interest from sports car enthusiasts, a dismal seven cars finding homes. In '68, Torix responded with a MkII edition, with the latest 104bhp Triumph engine, also adding the TXS and TXSS to the line-up. Mechanically identical to their older siblings, these new models were identifiable by the larger quarter-lights, and the fixed MGB rear screen, the TXSS model featuring a

Early TXS models used the Triumph GT6 engine, while later examples were fitted with four-cylinder Spitfire units.

The extreme TX Tripper sold in surprising numbers and seemingly caught the mood of the early '70s.

2.5-litre Triumph TR6 engine. In all, just ten TXSSs were built up until '76, some with donor car suspension rather than the Technical Exponents set-up, along with seven TX GTs, and three TXSs (a 1.3-litre Triumph-engined version offered in '71).

By the dawn of the '70s, Torix Bennett was becoming increasingly disillusioned with the motor industry. The stress of dealing with endless suppliers, and the hours spent deciphering the vagaries of Type Approval regulations, had taken their toll. Convalescing at his mother's home from a stomach ulcer, he hatched a plan to build a simple fun car that would appeal to hep cats rather than the string-back gloves brigade. The result stunned onlookers. The TX Tripper's styling was a halfway between a pseudo-beach buggy and a sports car, its one-piece, doorless body a riot of compound curves and bulges. The Tripper was launched at the '71 Racing Car Show, at Olympia, and was undeniably extreme, but, like the equally wacky Bond Bug, it managed to capture the mood of the time.

The Tripper's glassfibre body could be bolted on to any Spitfire or GT6 chassis, with an on-the-road price of around £1200. Bennett later built a demonstrator with a 2.5-litre straight-six unit under (and largely through) the bonnet, which propelled the flyweight machine to 60mph in 6.4 seconds. Unsurprisingly, the Tripper was to become the second most prolific seller in the company's history, with 48 bodies and 20 complete cars made up until '79. By this time, the firm was more engrossed (fittingly) in manufacturing bathtubs than building cars, although there were a couple of unsuccessful attempts to revive the model in the '80s. And though the Fairthorpe marque itself would be revived later that decade, under the Motorville banner, it died the death not long after, the Pathfinder (a heavily reworked Electron Minor) being way beyond its sell-by date.

In hardtop form, the Falcon
Caribbean was one of the
prettiest kits of its day.
(Malcolm McKay)

Falcon almost became a contender; so nearly made the quantum leap from being a maker of kits to becoming a fully-fledged motor manufacturer. But the company failed at the last hurdle. Falcon Shells was set up in 1957 by former Mulliner stylist Peter Pellandine, co-founder of Ashley Laminates, one of most prolific specials builders of the mid-'50s. Pellandine left Ashley armed with moulds for the company's Austin Seven and Ford Popular-based shells. At his Waltham Abbey facility, he used these moulds to produce shells, which he sold as the Falcon Mk1 and MkII respectively.

The curvaceous MkII bore more than a passing resemblance to a Jaguar D-type, and proved immensely popular with club racers when mated to Buckler, Cooper and, most successfully, Elva chassis. The works Austin-Healey equipe entered a Falcon-bodied Sprite in the 1960 Le Mans 24-hour classic, finishing twelfth overall and first in the 1000cc sports car class. The majority of shells, however, were used to create Ford specials, an effective, if time consuming, method of recycling a decrepit old saloon. To build a Falcon, it was first necessary to box the donor car's open channel-section members, remove three leaves from the front and rear transverse springs, discard the rear radius-arms, and replace the floor and gearbox cover with sheet aluminium, setting the floor below instead of above the frame. The builder then lowered the dynamo, raked the steering column, with the aid of a wedge, and replaced the radiator with a short crossflow unit. After this work had been completed, the chassis was ready to accept its new body. If such involved methods sounded unappealing to the customer, Falcon could provide a new, boxed-member Ford chassis to order but, in order to make

Falcon 515	
Made	Epping, Essex
Engine	Front-mounted, water-cooled 1498cc ohv 'four'
Construction	Multi-tubular semi-spaceframe chassis with bonded-on glassfibre body
Top speed	98mph
0–60mph	14 seconds
Price new	£1055 (1962)

an effective sports car, Pellandine suggested that a higher final-drive, a rear Panhard rod, independent front suspension and 15-inch wheels would be wise additions.

At £85 in 1959, the MkII shell was among the cheapest shells available, and relatively well made, with two pre-cut doors (Elva bodies had just the one), a lift-off bonnet, and the option of a curved Perspex racing screen, or a detachable hardtop with integral windscreen. That same year, Falcon introduced the MkIII, which was swiftly renamed the Caribbean. Initially offered as an open two-seater with a wrap around Vauxhall PA Cresta front screen, it was usually sold with a hardtop and, in this configuration, was undoubtedly one of the prettiest kits of the day. Initially with no side glazing of any kind, the Caribbean coupé gained sliding windows in 1961, evolving that same year into the MkIV, which had sliding glass in neat alloy frames. A restyled 'flowlined' bonnet, a new slatted grille, and a revised dashboard completed the makeover.

Towards the end of 1960, Falcon also unveiled the Bermuda. Again Ford based, this distinctive model was essentially a taller, wider four-seater variant of the Caribbean, with a crudely squared-off roof. Falcon offered its own substantial tubular frame, but found few takers, most customers opting for the original Ford item, or one of Laurie Bellamy's effective LMB chassis. In later years, Falcon tailored the Caribbean shell for the latter chassis, a logical progression, as there was increasing demand for easy-to-build kits that didn't require time-consuming cutting and shutting.

From 1962, Falcon offered kits with Len Terry's famed Terrier frames, that featured wishbone front suspension, and a live-axle located on radius-arms

Falcon Shells was set up in 1957 by former Mulliner stylist Peter Pellandine.

Falcon

Falcon's Competition bodyshell was used on a variety of chassis including this works Austin-Healey, which went on to win its class in the 1960 Le Mans 24-hour race.

and an A-bracket. This assembly could accept the latest 1340cc Ford Classic 'four' and, when sold with a completed body, was offered for £750, although relatively few were ever sold in this form. A further development was instigated around this time by respected tuner Dieter Glentzel (who was to later play a small but significant role in Ginetta's formative years). The German attempted to broker a deal to mate Caribbean bodies to front-wheel-drive DKW chassis and running gear, envisaging a production run of 1000 cars per year. A prototype was built, with an enlarged bonnet to allow improved engine accessibility, and a large radiator behind the block, with carburettor air intake via the front grille. When dispatched to Germany, the project bombed, after the antiquated chassis flexed, causing the doors to fly open when the car was driven on poorly paved surfaces. Had the scheme reached fruition, Pellandine had mooted setting up a factory in Northern Ireland to manufacture the car.

As the specials market started to ebb, Falcon changed direction, offering turn-key cars or partially built machines. But Pellandine was beginning to tire of the industry. He had one last stab at designing a new, complete sports car – the Peregrine. Built around the Terrier chassis, and powered by a 997cc Ford 105E engine, this attractive two-seater was launched in the spring of 1961, but never made it into full production. With an Austin-Healey Sprite costing under £700, there was no way the small Essex concern could compete on price, and just two cars were made, along with a backdoor shell made out-of-hours by a Falcon employee. It was later rumoured that this body had been used for the doomed MGB-powered Triton racing car.

In 1962, Pellandine sold the company to former sales manager Mike Moseley, and headed for Australia. However, Falcon was in a state of disarray,

The Falcon MkII bore a strong resemblance to a Jaguar D-Type, and proved popular with club racers.

the downturn in kit sales causing redundancies. The future looked bleak, but the new owner kept the firm afloat by diversifying into the industrial mouldings field, turning to the production of urns and window boxes among other things. In spite of this, car production was still very much to the fore, and Moseley initiated a new model to satisfy his desire to become a small-scale manufacturer of bespoke, hand-built cars, rather than just another kit-car outfit.

The attractive 515 coupé was unveiled to a receptive audience at the January 1963 London Racing Car Show, creating a media frenzy, Pathe News producing a film of a 515 being built in under two hours. Styled by Tom Rohonyi, a young Brazilian whom Moseley had met while Park Ward was trimming the DKW-Falcon, the 515's pleasing silhouette echoed the Jaguar E-type without being overly derivative. The glassfibre 'shell was bonded to the tubular chassis, designed by a moonlighting Lotus designer, and built by Progress Engineering. Power came from a 1500cc Ford pre-crossflow unit, with twin SU carburettors. The front suspension comprised a coil-spring and wishbone set-up, and the rear live-axle was located by trailing-arms, and coil-over-shock absorbers. The prototype boasted a Nash Metropolitan rear end,

The delightful Falcon Peregrine should have been a resounding success, but never made it into full production.

Falcon

47

which was substituted for a wider Ford affair on production cars. Priced at £845 in component form, or £1055 fully assembled, wire wheels were fitted as standard, and the cabin was lavishly equipped.

The arrival of the 515 coincided with a move to larger premises in Hatfield, which were soon filled, with nine different moulds required to produce bodies at the proposed rate of two a week; a rather optimistic figure as it transpired. In order to raise the car's profile, Australian racing driver Howden Ganley (later to compete in Formula 1 with BRM) was recruited to develop the 515, and lead a three-pronged assault on the '63 Le Mans 24-hour race. However, Falcon's entry was rejected, although Ganley campaigned a Coventry Climax-engined 515 with some success in national events.

For all the favourable press reports, Falcon wasn't exactly swamped with orders for its new baby, and in a boardroom coup in early '63, Moseley – then a minority shareholder – was unceremoniously sacked, his fellow directors preferring to cease moulding flowerpots, and the like, in order to concentrate solely on producing cars. This was a suicidal move that brought about a swift end, Falcon lurching into receivership in 1964. The assets from the motoring wing were bought by Marcos Cars, which shared a director with Falcon. Period figures quote a 515 production run of just 25 cars, although the actual number is believed to be around half that, including the original aluminium-bodied prototype crafted by Williams & Pritchard. Howden Ganley can only recall eight cars being made, one of them being transformed into an attractive convertible. Whatever the truth, it was a sad end for a once-prosperous marque that could have enjoyed major success had fate been kinder.

Tom Rohonyi-penned Falcon 515 was one of the prettiest of the early '60s specialist sports cars. Even so, it never sold in the numbers once envisaged.

The handsome Gilbern GT was Wales's only home-produced motor car during the early '60s.

Wales isn't renowned for its automobile industry, and during the '60s Gilbern *was* that industry. The marque was born in '59, when two enthusiasts of vastly disparate backgrounds joined forces to build a special. Bernard Friese, a German engineer, was employed by a firm that specialised in glassfibre mouldings. He had concocted a sports car that caught the attention of Giles Smith, a butcher, who had considered building a similar machine. The two joined forces to produce a more sophisticated version of Friese's one-off, Smith providing the premises in which to build it – a slaughterhouse in Church Village, near Pontypridd.

The success of their efforts prompted the duo to launch the car in kit-form, under the Gilbern (GILes BERNard) moniker. Each of the first two cars was supplied as a basic body/chassis unit, requiring the owners to source their own componentry. This arrangement did nothing to enhance the embryonic firm's reputation for build quality, so the decision was made to supply cars either as a comprehensive package with all-new mechanicals, or fully assembled. Similarly, the tiny Gilbern Sports & Components Ltd (later simplified to Gilbern Cars Ltd) could not hope to gain credibility with its existing location – chassis had to be lowered on to the street by a winch located in the workshop above the slaughterhouse so slightly more salubrious manufacturing works was found at the former Red Ash Colliery, near Llantwit Fardre.

Gilbern's first model, the GT, was a thoughtfully executed if not altogether attractive 2+2 coupé, competitively priced at £845 in component form. The car's one-piece glassfibre 'shell was riveted and bonded to its multi-tubular, semi-spaceframe chassis, early editions featuring wooden floorboards in the

Gilbern GT1800	
Made	Pontypridd, Glamorgan
Engine	Front-mounted, water-cooled 1798cc ohv 'four'
Construction	Multi-tubular perimeter chassis with glassfibre body
Top speed	107mph
0–60mph	12 seconds
Price new	£1261 (1965)

The GT was powered by a 948cc BMC A-Series 'four', available with an optional Shorrock supercharger.

boot and cabin, though these were swiftly substituted for glassfibre mouldings. The rear suspension initially utilised a Riley 1.5 axle supported on leaf springs and coil springs, with anti-tramp bars, a full-width Panhard rod, and telescopic shock absorbers. However, this set-up was soon dropped in favour of an axle located by trailing arms and a Panhard rod arrangement. The front end was suspended by a largely Austin-Healey Sprite-derived double-wishbone system, with nine-inch disc brakes offered as a £20 option. Steering was by worm and peg, robbed from the Austin A35.

The BMC parts bin also supplied the 948cc A-series 'four' that, when fitted with a Shorrock supercharger (a £70 extra), gave a top speed if 96mph at 6500rpm, and a 0–60mph time of 17.4 seconds. Other engines could be specified, including the highly-strung 1098cc ohc Coventry Climax FWA, or the 1622cc MGA B-series. The former didn't prove overly popular, the MG unit latterly becoming a standard fitment, receiving power hikes in parallel with the MGA. As with all specialist sports cars, specifications tended to change from one week to the next, so the GT received several cockpit revamps, the handsome wooden facias on the first batch soon making way for a padded black vinyl affair.

Annual GT production never came close to reaching triple figures. In its best year, 1962, Gilbern churned out 52 cars. Profits were marginal, a situation not aided by BMC's reluctance to supply parts at trade cost, Friese and Smith being forced to purchase componentry from local dealers. A switch to Ford V4 power proved a flop, all six cars so-equipped proving noisy and unrefined, which resulted in them being retrospectively converted to MG-spec. Although the cash flow proved more a trickle, the situation was alleviated to some degree with the formation of a dealer network in '62, under the auspices of former Lotus man Peter Cottrell.

The dependence on BMC continued unabated, Gilbern replacing the GT with the GT1800 in 1963. Unveiled at the London Racing Car Show, this new model appeared virtually identical to the car it replaced, but there were significant changes beneath the skin. The most important change was to the chassis, which was substantially stiffer thanks to additional triangulation at key stress areas. The car's 1799cc MGB engine was mounted further back in the frame for better weight distribution, which also freed up space for the adoption of rack-and-pinion steering. The MGB also provided its suspension, along with its front disc brakes, and 14-inch wire wheels. Tipping the scales at 2cwt less than its donor car, the GT1800 could top 110mph, and reach 60mph in a whisker over 12 seconds. *Motor* was moved to state that: 'Its performance keeps the Gilbern ahead of more deliberately-sporting vehicles.'

By 1965, Gilbern were producing around 150 cars a year, a remarkable achievement, as most of the workforce was drawn from the local mining communities. The reliance on BMC dealers for parts supply continued to blunt the profit margins. But Ford proved more hospitable, providing components at a reasonable price for the GT1800's replacement – the Genie. Debuting at the '66 Earls Court Motor Show, this latest model retained the basic concept of a multi-tubular semi-spaceframe with a one-piece glassfibre body, but was targeted at an altogether more discerning audience.

The Alfa Romeo GT Junior provided inspiration for the Gilbern Genie, seen here at Earls Court in 1966.

Invader production in 1970. The Invader was essentially an upmarket, reworked Genie.

Vastly different in appearance to its forebears, the Genie was more of a four-seater and less of a 2+2, the square-cut body aping that of the

Giorgetto Giugiaro-penned Alfa Romeo GT Junior. Ford had given Friese one of its new 60-degree V6 engines six months before the engine was officially announced for use in the Zephyr/Zodiac range, and it was this unit that was to power the new generation of Gilberns. The Genie was offered with this unit in 2.5-litre configuration, or in lightly tuned 3-litre form, which produced 141bhp, giving a top end of 120mph.

Initially the car proved a strong seller at £1425 but, between 1966 and '68, orders began to dry up as competition increased. The firm tried to respond by dropping the 2.5-litre option, and concentrating on improving the performance of the 3-litre model by fitting fuel-injection and various other tweaks. Renamed the P1 130, and boasting a claimed power output of 165bhp, this latest variant proved particularly unreliable, and most of the ten cars thus equipped were returned to the factory to have the original Weber carburettors refitted.

A pauperised Gilbern Cars was taken over in '68 by ACE Industrial Holdings Ltd of Cardiff, whose principal business was the manufacture of amusement arcade machines. Friese and Bernard resigned during the preceding six months, to be replaced by Maurice Collins and Mike Leather as joint directors. On the eve of the buy-out, Genie production had dwindled to less than 25 cars a year but, by mid-'69, it had steadily climbed to twice that figure. There were reasons to be cheerful, with the arrival of a new model being welcomed by the press and public alike.

Intended as a further move upmarket, the Invader was essentially a reworked Genie, with MGC front suspension and a more comprehensively stocked cabin. Gone was the vinyl-padded dash', replaced by a slab of veneered walnut, peppered with myriad instruments and switches. Electric windows, reclining front seats and rear bucket seats conspired to make the Invader a luxurious grand tourer, although the car's ride was on the harsh side of numbing, its only real flaw. Visually, there was little to tell it apart from its predecessor, save for the lightly restyled nose, but just to confuse punters, the factory had a habit of interchanging components or using up old parts stock, so some late Genies resembled early Invaders and vice versa.

At £1840, the Invader was pitched against some choice company, and wasn't the roaring success that its makers had hoped. As a result, the firm was bought out once more, by Clubmans Church, itself taken over almost immediately by Mecca Ltd. With precisely no interest in being part of the motor industry, Mecca sold Gilbern to former director Maurice Collins, who succeeded in doubling production but with little corresponding rise in profits.

By 1971, the Invader had been superseded by the MkII edition, the exact differences between the two being a mystery to even the most hardened marque devotees. The firm hedged its bets with the introduction of a sporting estate car variant of the Invader, pegged as a rival for the Ogle-designed Reliant Scimitar GT. Sadly, the ham-fisted styling did little to entice potential customers away from the Tamworth machine, and nor did the price tag which placed it uncomfortably close to a Jaguar E-type. Only 68 were built in total, along with a sole, second-hand Genie that was converted into a load-lugger at the factory.

The firm's financial woes were heightened by the crippling development costs sunk into an all-new mid-engined model that was to ultimately prove stillborn. TVR Trident and Elva GT160 stylist Trevor Fiore was partially responsible for the low-slung coupé's imposing silhouette and, had the car

The arrival of the Invader saw Gilbern briefly move into the big leagues, although the car was not the roaring success that its makers had hoped.

made it into production, it would have been powered by the unlikely BMC-Austin Maxi 1.5-litre unit. But the prototype never ran. Similarly, plans for a 3.4-litre, Westlake-Ford-powered Invader never made it out of the think tank, perhaps mercifully.

In 1972, Gilbern Cars moved on yet again, this time into the hands of Mike Leather, who had high hopes of reviving the firm's flagging fortunes. Hopes that were thwarted when the government introduced VAT and Special Car taxation. Liquidation seemed just a day or so away, but salvation – brief though it was – arrived in the shape of management consultant and Invader driver Roger Solway. Later that year Solway signed on as a trouble-shooter, just as the Invader MkIII was introduced.

The arrival of the MkIII marked the first significant makeover for a body style that was now eight years old. New moulds were made, and the front-end styling, with its broad grille cavity and wide wheel arch extensions, gave the car an infinitely more aggressive appearance. Underneath the new body, larger, square-section tubing at the front housed a complete Ford Cortina subframe, complete with brakes, suspension and steering rack. At the rear was a modified Cortina Estate axle, with a Ford Taunus differential. Power came from a Capri 3000GT V6, mated to a four-speed 'box with overdrive top. Gilbern claimed a 130mph top speed, and a 0–60mph time of 7.2

seconds. However, with a price tag of a lofty £2693 in '72, the MkIII couldn't hope to compete with mass-produced rivals, despite now being entirely hand-built, the home-assembly option being no longer available.

Leather had been keen to tempt overseas interest, and six left-hand-drive MkIIIs were distributed across Europe to act as demonstrators but, despite an order for 150 cars from a Dutch dealer, the writing was on the wall. Reading it with objectivity, Leather knew that the coffers were never likely to be replenished, and on July 9, 1973, the receivers were called in. The 50-strong staff were laid off three days later.

Over the course of the next twelve months, numerous attempts were made to revive the marque, but to no avail. Eventually, millionaire enthusiast Anthony Peters purchased the dormant firm, and managed to shift three more MkIIIs, although the firm ceased trading almost immediately having accrued debts of around £100,000. Peters's controlling share in the firm was bought by a consortium of London-based accountants and businessmen, whose interest in the firm was never made public. All remaining stock disappeared almost overnight, while many of the firm's records were destroyed. This was a sad and shadowy end for a marque that instilled national pride in its homeland: a rare feat in itself.

Late examples of the Invader were only offered in fully-built form, but the hefty price tag led to the marque's demise.

Ginetta

The Ginetta G4 was a beautifully styled little sportster, which saw Ginetta make the leap from specials builder to respected motor manufacturer.

'Ginetta – the best-known car company you've never heard of.' A quote attributed to an American scribe that makes no real sense, yet perfectly encapsulates the marque. Mention of the name invariably draws blank faces even in its homeland, but, to a small band of cognoscenti, the company is a national treasure. This little-known minnow was in the charge of four brothers – Bob, Douglas, Trevers and Ivor Walklett – for the first 31 of its 40-plus years in business.

It was Ivor who subsequently blamed himself for getting his brothers embroiled in the motor industry. The youngest of the four, he had been swept along by enthusiasm for the 'specials' movement, building his own one-off machine in the mid-'50s, said to have resembled a Maserati 4CLT. Based on the mechanics of a pre-war Wolseley Hornet, this spartan machine led a brief and inauspicious existence, coming to a sticky end after connecting with a tree stump in the driveway of the Walklett family home.

His pride, if not his car, undented, Ivor set to work on building a further special, this time a tubular-spaceframe design clad with simple aluminium sheet bodywork. Like so many similar machines, this latest effort used unmodified Ford E93A components, so performance wasn't exactly electrifying, although the car handled admirably thanks to the addition of telescopic dampers and modified front radius arms.

Late in '57, when Ivor was nearing the end of his National Service, his special proved a major draw, and it didn't take long for one of his local RAF acquaintances to request that another body and chassis assembly be made in order to create a replica. Ivor roped in his brothers, who were running an agricultural engineering firm in Suffolk, to prepare the kit package, inspiring

Ginetta G4	
Made	Witham, Essex
Engine	Front-mounted, water-cooled 997cc ohv 'four'
Construction	Multi-tubular spaceframe with glassfibre body
Top speed	105mph
0–60mph	10.5 seconds
Price new	£514 (1961)

them to officially launch the car for general sale in January '58. Dubbed the Ginetta G2 (the Wolseley special was posthumously awarded the title G1), as many as 100 of these Lotus 6-esque roadsters were sold over the next two years. Advertised at £156 ex-works, a G2 could have been put on the road for as little as £250.

Flushed with the success of their fledgling enterprise, the brothers (Ivor had, by this time, joined full-time) pressed on with two new designs. The first was the G3, a conventional kit car with a square-tube spaceframe. A split E93A front beam axle was used, with coil springs and dampers, to give an independent front suspension set-up. Outwardly, the car's silhouette was pleasing enough, if a little innocuous, and the glassfibre bodyshell was well made and easy to piece together. Introduced in 1959, the G3 was offered for two years, and around 60 were made, including some sold as bare shells to be fitted onto proprietary chassis under the Fairlite moniker.

It was the arrival of the G4 that saw Ginetta make the leap from specials builder to respected motor manufacturer. This achingly pretty little sportster was launched without a fanfare in late-'60, before taking its public bow, to rapturous applause, at the following January's Racing Car Show. There was

The Ginetta G4 made its public debut at the '61 Racing Car Show to rapturous applause.

G4s proved giant killers in club racing, and Norman Moffet was one the model's key exponents, scooping two consecutive Irish Sports Car crowns. (The roof bulge mercifully was not standard.)

Ginetta was at the forefront of the '60s customer racing car business, this model being a G18 Formula Ford.

nothing especially radical about the car's appearance or construction, but it perfectly epitomised that old maxim, 'If it looks right, it is right.'

The G4 used a spaceframe chassis with low sides (to allow the use of conventional doors), and was clothed in a glassfibre 'shell comprising several moulded sections. Power was originally to have come from Coventry Climax's rev-happy FWA 'four', in short-stroke 742cc configuration, but there were several drawbacks to using this engine, the principal problem being that the engine would have been intolerably noisy for road use. It would also prove necessary to source gearboxes and rear axle assemblies from other suppliers, rather than acquiring a complete drive-train package from just one manufacturer. Ultimately, the FWA engine never made it into series production, the Walkletts opting for a 997cc Ford 105E unit that produced 39.5bhp at 5000rpm – which, in a car weighing only 8.75cwt, meant a top speed of 105mph, and 0–50mph in nine seconds.

Attention to detail was rife, the G4 featuring a full undertray to aid air penetration, double-skinned doors, and a scuttle sculptured to accept an Austin-Healey Sprite Mk1 windscreen (as used on the G3). Though stark to the point of austerity, the car's cabin did at least boast a full compliment of instruments, leather-covered, alloy-spoked VW Derrington steering wheel, and thoughtful storage bins incorporated into the doors.

Priced at £697 in comprehensive kit-form with full weather equipment, the G4 was pitched directly at the Lotus 7, which though marginally cheaper, couldn't compete in terms of specification or build quality. Early customers were swift to exploit the car's handling prowess, and Fos Wilson, Ian and Malcolm Douglas, along with Ivor Walklett himself, took to the track with some success. The '62 season saw young engineer Nick Grace join the fray, and he became one of the stars of British domestic sports car racing the following year with his Martin-tuned G4. Grace regularly beat Merlyn Mk4A sports-racer driver, and future F1 runner, Piers Courage, among others.

Fortified by the G4's popularity, the Walkletts felt confident enough to concentrate solely on car production, ending their involvement in agricultural engineering with the move to a new manufacturing facility in Witham, Essex, in mid-'62. The move coincided with the first of many G4 developments. The new 1498cc Ford pre-crossflow engine was offered in an otherwise unchanged G4, which was re-christened the G5, for £525. The G5 nomenclature was dropped almost immediately, as customers couldn't outwardly tell the difference between the two models, and nor, for that matter, could the brothers. To avoid confusion, it was subsequently referred to as the G4-1500.

The car's styling also came in for a makeover, and a new, detachable 'Series 2' tail section was offered for £15. The existing short tail was extended by a further eight inches, and the Lotus Eleven-like tail fins were severely cropped, and curved downwards to a blunt panel that was à la mode at the time. Aside from making the G4 appear even more attractive, the new and perfectly formed rump was also more practical, boot capacity being increased. The S2 tail became standard equipment from '64, as did an Austin A40 rear axle in place of the previous Ford Anglia unit, giving a wider track and revised gearing. The front suspension was also reworked, with the lower wishbones repositioned to improve the car's ride.

Bob Walklett had long been keen to publicise the marque in Europe. A tie-in with German tuning legend Albrecht Mantzel, to jointly develop a car with which to mount a challenge for class honours in the '63 Nürburgring 1000km race should have been mutually beneficial. But it wasn't. It was agreed that a G4 employing one of Mantzel's demon 850cc DKW Junior two-strokes would have a serious chance of winning the hotly contested up-to-1000cc category. Designated the G6, the new car featured a ZF 'box with a special alloy bellhousing. Without any time to test the car, the G6 prototype was dispatched by air-freight from London Heathrow to Frankfurt. On arrival in Germany, the car was taken directly to the Nürburgring where the engine was fitted.

Mantzel's team installed a hefty steel fuel tank in the boot, and were forced to run an ungainly (and tall) windscreen in practice, drivers Peter Ruby and Mantzel's son Dieter discovering serious handling problems. Bob Walklett was called for advice, and he caught the next available flight to Frankfurt. On arrival at the track, he discovered that the vast weight of the fuel tank had compressed the rear springs to the point that that there was no longer any suspension travel. With no time to install a lighter glassfibre tank, the car lined up on the grid for the start. Recording a top speed of 117mph, the foam-grey roadster later suffered fuel-starvation at the far side of the track.

The beautifully proportioned G15 was briefly a roaring success, but proved a victim of outside forces.

Regulations didn't permit outside assistance, so the Ginetta's race was over.

This was not altogether the end of the G6 project. A few more cars were converted, and Mantzel retained a British racing green example for his own use, while the Nürburgring car passed into the hands of Swiss hillclimber Alfred Junker, who modified it out of all recognition, switching to a 1.2-litre Cosworth-Ford screamer, and junking the live rear axle in favour of a bespoke independent arrangement incorporating Lotus and Triumph parts. Ginetta itself devised a further variation on the theme, with an independent rear suspension arrangement of its own, plus a rear-mounted gearbox, but this project, dubbed the G7, was dropped as other ventures took precedence.

By 1964, Ginetta was involved in myriad schemes, some more successful than others. First there was an all-new independent rear suspension set-up for the regular G4, Chris Meek campaigning the works 'G4R' (the R tag predictably standing for racing) with aplomb. And then there was the G8 Formula 3 car. A novel and exceedingly attractive machine, this open-wheeler was designed to compete in the new one-litre series, and featured a distinctive plastic monocoque; two shells bonded over a steel perimeter chassis, a time and labour-intensive build process. The car displayed admirable rigidity, and Meek campaigned the factory-entered prototype towards the end of the season at Snetterton, finishing fourth on its debut. But with insufficient time to develop the project any further, and with a down-on-power Holbay-tuned engine, the G8 adventure was soon over. A Formula 2 variant, the G9, barely made it off the drawing board.

At the January '65 Racing Car Show, Ginetta unleashed its G10. Aimed squarely at the Stateside market, this sophisticated roadster featured a 4727cc Ford V8 motor aboard a tubular-steel chassis. Suspension was independent all-round by double wishbones and coil springs, the specification justifying the car's hefty £2750 price tag. A devilishly attractive machine, the car's shape was to some extent dictated by the use of MGB doors and windscreen. Even so, Ivor Walklett managed to produce a silhouette that any Italian styling house would have been happy to put its name to. The prototype was raced by Chris Meek at Brands Hatch the following November, winning a thrilling battle with Robbie Gordon's ex-Dick Protheroe, Malcolm Sayer-smoothed Jaguar 'Lightweight' E-type, which represented the very best in British GT racers at that time.

It was this success that prompted Ginetta's US distributor, George Kipps, to place an order for six left-hand-drive G10s. With Ford agreeing to supply engines and transmissions, sales success for this newcomer seemed a mere formality. Unfortunately, the car hadn't been homologated for the Sports Car Club of America's racing series, in which Kipps planned to field a car to gain some publicity, so the G10 would be forced to move up a class and compete head-on with McLaren and Lola sports-racers. Against such competition, it would have been completely out-classed, and there was little chance of the firm producing the requisite 100 cars in a year to satisfy the regulations. Reluctantly, the American cancelled his order. The project was canned after two convertibles and four closed cars had been completed.

Not easily discouraged, the Walkletts redesigned the car for the home market. While physically similar, the G11 was very different beneath the skin. This latest variant used a square-tube backbone chassis, and the front suspension used proven double wishbones derived from the Triumph Vitesse, while at the rear an MGB live axle was located by an A-frame and radius arms, with coil springs and telescopic dampers. The Ford V8 was substituted for the 1.8-litre MGB B-series 'four'.

Again offered in open and closed configurations, the G11 was a stylish sports car capable of 110mph in total civility, and looked set to enjoy a long and successful production run. Unfortunately, the reliance on BMC for the supply of MG components proved to be the G11's downfall. Without fail, BMC would be late with deliveries – when it would deliver at all. On one occasion, there were six G11s awaiting doors and, after two months of waiting, BMC delivered twelve left-hand doors and no right-hand ones! With such a parts supply, the G11 was doomed to an early grave. With hindsight, Bob Walklett kicked himself for committing the company to producing a car that stood no chance of gaining support from BMC, as it was after all a direct, if exclusive, rival to the MGB.

That would have been the end of the G11 had it not been for the efforts of enthusiast Russell Madden. Already the owner of a G4, he became infatuated with the G11 on visiting Ginetta's Witham works. Though the car was now out of production, Madden persuaded Bob Walklett to relinquish all the unused chassis, on the proviso that the firm would produce new bodies as and when he needed them. A handful were produced through to the mid-'70s.

These regrettable experiences in the road car sector saw the Walkletts redirect their efforts back to the race track with the exquisite G12 sports-racer. Introduced in 1966, this diminutive machine briefly ruled the roost in domestic GT racing, in the hands of Chris Meek, *Motoring News* editor Ian Tee and Willie Green. The latter took eleven wins from twelve starts that season, breaking the lap record at every circuit he visited. Not that there was anything particularly special about the design; it just worked 'straight out of the box'. Underneath the pretty glassfibre skin lay a spaceframe chassis with the centre body section bonded on for additional stiffness. The front end was suspended

The G16 Group 6 car, seen here at the '69 BOAC 500 at Brands Hatch, was never fully developed.

by double wishbones, and at the rear, single top links with lower reversed wishbones, and double radius arms were used. Green's car sported a 1-litre Formula 2 Cosworth SCA engine amidships, although other engines could be accommodated. John Burton campaigned a 2-litre Martin V8-engined example, but it proved unreliable, while Green would later upgrade to a Lotus twin-cam four-pot. Around 28 G12s were built in two years, and many of them were subsequently converted for road use after their competition lives were over.

While G12 production was in full swing, the G4 had come in for further revisions. In late-'65, the decision was made to switch from round to square-section chassis tubing, saving on materials, while adding further rigidity. More significant was the adoption of purpose-made upper and lower wishbones in place of the previous Triumph Herald items. The following year saw a new 'Series 3' restyle. The familiar (and rather lovely) one-piece bonnet was replaced with a new frontal treatment that incorporated pop-up headlamps similar in appearance to the Lamborghini Miura's. Further alterations included a more-rounded windscreen and the addition of exterior door handles, with the option of a chromium-plated front bumper (a modified rear Volkswagen Beetle article). The cabin now featured such niceties as carpeting and sound deadening. However, the trackside dominance of the G12 saw Ginetta production up to full capacity trying to satisfy demand, while future models were undergoing development. G4 production dwindled to nothing, the final car being delivered in May '67. The G14 – there never was a G13 for superstitious reasons – was conceived as a G4 replacement, with a backbone chassis, 1.6-litre Ford engine, and a body aping the lines of the G10, albeit scaled down.

However, this project was abandoned before the prototype had even been constructed due to fears of high insurance rates hitting sales. The decision was made to build a car with a smaller engine, the 875cc Sunbeam Imp Sport-powered G15 debuting at the '67 Earls Court Motor Show. The G15 was a beautifully proportioned machine, the Imp engine, transaxle and trailing arms mounted under the upswept rear of a square-section tubular-steel chassis, while the front end was suspended by a double wishbone arrangement (derived from the Triumph Spitfire). Tipping the scales at a whisker below 10cwt, and with 55bhp on tap, the tiny coupé could top 100mph.

A year would pass before Ginetta was in a position to deliver any cars, the public debut proving a little premature. Among the changes made before production started was the relocation of the radiator from the rear to the nose of the car. Advertised at £799 in component form, the G15 initially proved a strong seller, but the Walkletts were still keen to maintain a presence in motor racing. The G16 Group 6 sports-racer of '68 was a successor to the G12, designed to accept 2-litre motors from BMW, BRM, Cosworth and Coventry Climax. But the brothers were embroiled in numerous other projects, so this handsome design was never fully developed. The works G16A-BRM was campaigned with marginal success by Bev Bond, while John Burton's Worcestershire Racing Organisation machine competed on the Continent but could not keep pace with rival Chevrons.

As the '60s drew to a close, Ginetta returned to open-wheel single-seaters with the Imp-engined Formula 4, which found its métier on the hills, especially when driven by Peter Voight. A Formula Ford version, the G18, proved an also-ran, while a G19 Formula 3 car design was later abandoned. More ambitious still was Ginetta's proposed entry into the elite world of Formula 1. Bob Walklett had negotiated with BRM's Wilkie Wilkinson for the supply of a 3-litre V12, with the intention of fielding a car during the '69 season. Perhaps predictably, this grandiose plan came to naught after only a few castings had been made.

The G15 was now well established, with the optional 998cc 'S' edition only heightening its appeal. Success on the track with Barry Wood's works-sponsored car, and Alison Davis's similar Femfresh-liveried car, meant that Ginetta maintained its profile in racing, although there were to be no more purpose-built racers until the lacklustre G22 Sports 2000 car of the late-'70s. Plans for a restyled G12 road car, with 3-litre power (the G20, the tag also shared with the aborted F1 car), were abandoned for fear of pricing it out of the market, the brothers pressing on with the graceful G21 coupé.

Unveiled at the 1970 Earls Court Motor Show, the delicious front-engined G21 was aimed squarely at the Marcos, TVR and Gilbern market, and represented a shift in company policy. The G21 was a car for the keen driver who had no motor sport aspirations: this wasn't a thinly disguised racer, but

With the G21, Ginetta aimed to take on TVR: it failed though the model was superior to anything made in Blackpool at the time.

a dignified tourer. Underneath the Ivor Walkett-penned body lay a ladder-type chassis, similar to the G15's, but with a transmission tunnel. Powering the prototype was a 1.6-litre Ford 'four', but this was dropped in favour of a 1725cc Sunbeam unit, with the option of an H120 Holbay-tuned 'S' version of Ford's 3-litre V6 engine.

Though the G21 was enthusiastically received, the vagaries of Type Approval and rigorous crash testing (the car was never offered in kit form) meant that production didn't get underway until June '73, within a new 40,000sq ft manufacturing facility in Sudbury, Suffolk. Unfortunately, this timing coincided neatly with the arrival of VAT, the fuel crisis, and the three-day working week. G15 production ended in '74, as the Imp engine was no longer manufactured and, with few products to sell, Ginetta came perilously close to going to the wall.

The firm relocated back to its old Witham premises, offering the G21 as late as 1978, although the last car (number 68) was built two years earlier. The firm survived the '70s, supplying spares for existing cars, in addition to making a small batch of air-cooled VW-powered G15s for the US market, before making a major comeback in the '80s with a series of kit-form saloons and utility vehicles. And, although the firm passed into new hands in '89, Ivor Walklett has returned to building new G4s and G12s through his DARE UK concern, primarily for the voracious Japanese market.

Gordon-Keeble

The Gordon-Keeble was styled by 21-year-old Giorgetto Giugiaro, and the steel bodies for the prototypes were built by Bertone, although production cars were fitted with glassfibre 'shells.

If you could extract the essence of pure styling by removing all the usual compromises – populist moves and clumsy detailing – you would be left with an unembellished yet exceedingly beautiful automobile. That is the theory, and the Gordon-Keeble comes close to proving the ideal. Born from the ashes of the Peerless project, this exquisite machine's star shone all too briefly. That it achieved such dismal commercial failure, only adds to the pathos.

Engineer Jim Keeble was approached by American serviceman Rick Nielsen, with a request to install a small-block Chevrolet V8 in a Peerless. Unbeknown to Keeble, Peerless MD John Gordon had envisaged building a similar car and, realising that the firm was about to crash, entered discussions with a view to Keeble designing an all-new machine – the Gordon GT.

Work commenced on the chassis in November 1959, Gordon insisting that the car should be a full four-seater, with a wheelbase of 102in and a track of 52in. Constructed entirely of square-section steel tubing, the spaceframe aped that of the Peerless. At the rear, a de Dion axle was located by two parallel links, held in place laterally by a Watt's linkage and coil springs.

While Keeble was engrossed in building the chassis, Gordon travelled to Italy to meet with Nuccio Bertone and his latest recruit, Giorgetto Giugiaro. A deal was struck with little more than a handshake – Carrozzeria Bertone would build the body, with the 21-year-old wunderkind responsible for the styling, the only stipulation being that it should have four headlights.

By mid-January 1960, the chassis was completed and loaded aboard a transporter bound for Turin, in order to be clothed in its new Latin body. The completed car was scheduled to be delivered to the March '60 Geneva Salon but, on press day, John Gordon was marooned on an empty stand – the

Gordon-Keeble	
Made	Slough, Buckinghamshire
Engine	Front-mounted, water-cooled 5363cc ohv V8
Construction	Semi-spaceframe with glassfibre body
Top speed	140mph
0–60mph	7.5 seconds
Price new	£2798 (1964)

prototype was stuck at a customs post between Italy and Switzerland. After hectic negotiations, the car was released, and it proved the undoubted star of the event despite being a non-runner, missing its fuel tank, exhaust and wiring.

Though buoyed by the car's rapturous reception, Gordon realised that Peerless Motors Ltd was in no fit state to build cars in any volume. The writing was on the wall, so Gordon re-registered the prototype in his own name shortly before the firm's inevitable demise, in order to fend off the receivers. He immediately formed the Gordon Automobile Company and, desperate for operating capital, sold a stake in the project to a nearby furniture retailer.

The original plan called for GT bodies and chassis to be produced in Italy at a rate of 20 per week, with final assembly to be carried out at a new Slough facility. Production would commence in September '60 with 25 cars being built in the first month, rising to 250 by December of that year. Sadly, these figures were to prove extremely optimistic.

During a press launch for the car in the summer of 1960, Gordon met George Wansborough, a senior board member of Mercantile Credit and rabid car fan, who occasionally wrote road tests for the *Financial Times*. Still desperately in need of funding, Gordon invited Wansborough to become a director of the fledgling firm in the hope that he might be able to use his contacts to find a backer.

Equally pressing was the need to ensure a steady supply of engines. The following spring, Gordon accompanied the prototype GT aboard the *Queen Elizabeth* for a round of meetings with senior General Motors personnel, including old friend Zora Arkus Duntov, universally recognised as the father of the Chevrolet Corvette. After stringing together several spirited laps around GM's Detroit test track, Duntov gave his blessing to the project, and

Giugiaro's original rendering of the Gordon GT. Gordon's only stipulation was that the car should have four headlights.

Gordon G.T.

Body by Bertone

The Gordon GT making its Geneva debut in March 1960. The car received a rapturous reception.

introduced Gordon to Ed Cole, the sports car-loving executive vice president of General Motors. On the strength of a blast through Michigan's back roads, Cole agreed to supply Gordon with the latest Corvette V8 engine and gearbox for an all-inclusive £400 – an unprecedented move, as this was the first time that GM had officially sanctioned the supply of powerplants to an outside manufacturer.

If that was not enough, Cole asked Gordon to build 1500 GTs which could be displayed in Chevrolet dealerships to create 'showroom traffic'. Leaving for England after three months in the States with spirits high, there was bad news for Gordon awaiting his return; Wansborough had still to find a backer. However, Nuccio Bertone mentioned that Italian refrigeration magnate Renzo Rivolta was looking to move into the luxury car market, and

The Gordon-Keeble's dashboard resembled an aircraft flightdeck.

proposed a meeting. Gordon drove the prototype to Milan, where Rivolta requested he borrow a chassis for evaluation. Much to the Englishman's dismay, talks between both parties came to nothing, the wealthy Italian launching the Iso Rivolta coupé, which was physically similar to the Gordon GT, in '64. Indeed, so close was the cribbing that *Autocar* commented on the car's launch: 'In most fundamentals, the resemblance between this newcomer and the original Gordon GT prototype of 1960 seems more than coincidental.'

After all his efforts to secure finance had failed, Wansborough took the plunge and sank his own money into the venture so as to at

Chevrolet provided its 327cu in pushrod V8 for the production version of the Gordon-Keeble.

least get production up and running. In mid-'63, a decrepit factory at Southampton airport was purchased, and an assembly line was installed. By this time, the decision had been made to manufacture bodies from glassfibre rather than steel and, by March of the following year, a paltry nine shells had been completed and mated to their frames.

The car was effectively relaunched in front of the press at the Savoy Hotel on December 10, 1963, as the Gordon-Keeble GK1. Sales slowly trickled along, customers receiving a delightfully twee, if slightly surreal owner's handbook, which was full of useful advice including such gems as: 'Treat your car initially as you would the contents of your cellar – gently and in moderation. Don't start up a cold engine and then leave it idling while you rush indoors to pay a belated farewell to your wife. In the interests of minimum engine wear, skip the farewell and drive away. When facing the music on your return in the evening, make a mental note henceforth to adopt a definite sequence of events prior to your morning departure. You will achieve substantially diminished wear from your engine, and deserve greater affection from your wife.'

Aside from the switch to glassfibre bodies, the other principal change between prototype and production cars was the move to the new 5.3-litre, 327cu in Chevrolet V8, after General Motors ceased production of its aged solid-tappet 4.6-litre 'eight'. Producing around 300bhp at 5100rpm, the larger displacement motor was fed by a single Carter carburettor in place of the triple Rochester set-up of the earlier powerplant. Physical differences amounted to little more than chrome window surrounds, the mildly revised cabin, with its elaborate centre console, resembling an aircraft flight deck.

By now, the GK1 sported an unusual tortoise logo on its snout, the origins of this motif almost as bizarre as the contents of the owner's handbook. During a brochure photo-shoot, Gordon wanted to demonstrate the car's luggage capacity, and proceeded to load several suitcases into the boot for the benefit of the photographer. The Great Train Robbery had taken place only a few days earlier, and Gordon's loading exercise was witnessed by an old

The Gordon-Keeble was a masterpiece of automotive architecture, and this rear three-quarter view shows the car's classic lines.

woman, who promptly called the police in the belief that she was watching an exchange of loot. As the officers carried out their investigation, a tortoise walked in front of the car. It was picked up and placed on the bonnet for a spur-of-the-moment picture and immediately lost bowel control, its urine stripping the paint!

By February 1965, the coffers were empty, the situation made worse by a strike at Adwest which supplied the steering boxes. With 16 cars awaiting delivery, but lacking these vital parts, there was no money coming in, and half the workforce had to be laid off, the rest being made redundant two months later as the receivers were called in. A rescue venture was plotted by motor traders Harold Smith and Geoffrey West, and production hesitantly got under way in a former light bulb factory in Sholing, but just seven cars were made under the new regime before the project foundered in the summer of '66. Just 99 GK1s had been made.

But that wasn't altogether the end of the Gordon-Keeble. Sports car enthusiast John de Bruyne – who had once been a shareholder in Diva – bought the last few remaining assets, hatching grandiose plans to revive the car under his own name. He immediately engaged Peter Fluck (better known for initiating the satirical *Spitting Image* TV show) to restyle the car; a rather misguided move as, to many people, the results were infinitely inferior to Giugiaro's timeless original. Gone was the 'Chinese eye' frontal treatment, and in its place were four, conventionally arranged headlights, while the rear end was squared-off with repellent Ford Zodiac MkIV tail light clusters. While the body was massaged into ugliness, few mechanical changes were made. The de Bruyne Grand Touring appeared at the New York Show, a trade event for car dealers, but the would-be motor mogul canned the project shortly thereafter, due to the complexities of the car's construction. With it died the Grand Sport, an equally ungainly low-slung mid-engined coupé in the De Tomaso Mangusta idiom. A sad and ignoble end for a marque which deserved to be exalted rather than pitied.

GSM

The GSM Delta was much-favoured by clubman racers in the early '60s.

South Africa isn't exactly renowned for its sports cars, but undoubtedly the best known is the GSM Delta, which was conceived, of all places, in a lock-up garage in Earls Court, London. Bob van Niekirk and Willie Meisner had long harboured dreams of building their own line of sports cars, and travelled to England in the mid-'50s to learn about the intricacies of glassfibre. In 1957, they set to work designing a simple ladder-frame, made from tubing used for irrigation pipes, mated to modified Ford 100E running gear. The front suspension used cut-down MacPherson struts as kingpins, and the coil springs were replaced by a transverse leaf spring, an unorthodox idea that worked surprisingly well. The donor Ford's rear axle sported welded-on coil-over-shock absorbers, and was located by trailing arms and an A-bracket.

Niekirk and Miesner roped in fellow Springbok Verster de Witt, a senior Rootes stylist, to pen a body for the chassis. The first 'shell was completed in April '57 and was promptly sold for £75 to raise funds to ship the moulds back to Cape Town, where the partners formed the Glassport Motor Company. The first two completed Dart cars were equipped with Willment-tuned 1172cc Ford sidevalve engines, debuting at a race at Gunner's Circle, near Cape Town, and promptly winning. Fortified by this success, and with a full order book, the partners bought a larger factory and, by the end of 1959, 41 cars had found homes. GSM Darts swiftly became the car of choice for the clubman racer, the most notable success being overall victory in the '59 Kyalami Nine Hours.

Having found a niche in motor sport, GSM then targeted the enthusiast looking for something a little more civilised. Owners started to demand road

An early GSM Delta, minus any weather gear, competing in the '58 Ford Specials race at Snetterton.

John Bramfield's GSM with ugly factory hard-top leads Marcos and Abarth at Goodwood, 1963.

cars with a windscreen and some semblance of weather protection. The enterprising pair created a hardtop with a cut-down Ford Zephyr windscreen that did nothing for the car's looks and found few takers, de Witt producing another roof in swift succession, with a reverse-slope back window à la Ford Anglia 105E.

Meanwhile, Meisner returned to England and found a backer to set up production in the UK. Moulds and jigs were shipped to Southampton, but the would-be sponsor was in jail on their arrival, having been found guilty of numerous financial irregularities. But a good Samaritan arrived in the shape of John Scott who set the South African partners a challenge. He and his partners would stump up enough money to commence production, if de Witt and Meisner could build a car to win a race at Brands Hatch on April 18, 1960 – a tall order, as the race was just ten days away. They succeeded.

A factory was set up in West Malling, Kent, but a name change was deemed in order, as a bicycle manufacturer owned the rights to the Dart tag. After much deliberation, Scott came up with Delta. A switch to 997cc Ford 105E power provided the car with a credible turn of speed and it wasn't long before more powerful engines were substituted, including large Ford units along with Coventry Climax, Alfa Romeo, and even Porsche 'fours'. In competition, works-assisted driver Jeff Uren scooped Class A of the '61 Production Sports Car Championship, by which time as many as four cars were leaving the production line per week.

Unfortunately, racing proved costly, and the development of a new fastback variant, bodied in aluminium by Williams & Pritchard, cost the firm dearly. The

GSM Delta	
Made	West Malling, Kent
Engine	Front-mounted, water-cooled 997cc ohv 'four'
Construction	Ladderframe with glassfibre body
Top speed	95mph
0–60mph	14 seconds
Price new	£1250 (1961)

The South African-made GSM Flamingo coupé complete with distinctive 'dorsal fin'.

Piet van Niekerk campaigning his GSM Flamingo at Kyalami, 1964.

coffers ran dry, and the firm slipped into receivership in late-'61, despite a large number of orders outstanding. Around 60 Deltas had been built, along with the two fastback prototypes. Meisner had returned to South Africa the previous year, opening a service station and keeping GSM production as a sideline. Bob van Niekirk followed not long after, with a vision for a new luxury coupé – the Flamingo.

With help from Verster de Witt, van Niekerk took a reject Dart body and created a new fastback roof-line, incorporating an Austin A40 'Farina' windscreen, and a distinctive dorsal fin between the rear screens. The front end was restyled using Porsche 356 headlights and an augmented grille cavity. The chassis remained as before, aside from the adoption of Mini 'doughnuts' with inboard rockers to compress them, a trick later adopted by Grand Prix teams. Ford's enduring pre-crossflow motor provided power. But production never amounted to more than a leisurely trickle, with around 128 Flamingos produced up until '64 when GSM folded. A last gasp 225cu in Ford V8-powered car apparently scared the financier, and that effectively spelt the end of the marque, for a while at least.

In 1998, GSM enthusiast Les Hayden bought the production rights to the Dart, and reintroduced the roadster to an appreciative South African market. The Hayden Dart is a kit car in the truest sense, requiring the customer to source all componentry from a Ford Escort Mk2. The styling has also received a makeover, large fender flares being required for the wider track. There is also a none-too-subtle front bib spoiler, a rather misguided move to update what was always a clean shape. Though only marketed in its homeland at present, there is talk of exports to the UK and America in the future.

As a final footnote to the story, the very first GSM body, sold to raise funds to ship the moulds back to South Africa back in '57, led a chequered existence. The bare 'shell was bought by Donald Parker to clothe his Nimbus Special hillclimber. Powered by the ubiquitous 1172cc Ford sidevalve 'four', driving via a chain and a Norton motorcycle transmission to a solid axle with no differential, it was apparently lethal at anything above pottering speeds. After the car made several attempts at killing its creator, it was comprehensively revamped, but retained the Dart body, albeit heavily modified. Ultimately, the car ended up with a rear-mounted 1275cc Mini Cooper S A-series, with a whopping Wade supercharger, churning out around 150bhp. With an all-in weight of just 8cwt, it was blessed with a power-to-weight ratio of an amazing 375bhp per tonne – when it didn't succeed in melting its pistons. The car still exists in the hands of Parker's brother-in-law, Mike Hentall.

LE MANS COUPE
GT CONVERSION

ENGINEERED FOR SPEED WITH COMFORT AND SAFETY

Lenham's Spridget fastback conversion proved a huge success, seen here with the attractive Le Mans bonnet.

Flick through any late-'60s copy of *Hot Car* or *Cars & Car Conversions* and, among the classifieds for fur-lined seat covers and stick-on go-faster stripes, you will invariably spot a small advertisement for Lenham Motor Company hard-tops. A Lenham lid was de rigeur for any self-respecting sports car owner, but there was more to this small but enterprising Kent firm than just glassfibre add-ons.

Marque founder Julian Kingsford-Booty began dabbling in the motor trade during the late-'50s. A photographer for Hunter Penrose by day, he dealt in historic machinery by night. He soon reached the stage where taking photographs was getting in the way of trading in cars, so he made a break for it in '62, forming the Vintage & Sports Car Garage on the proceeds of a vintage Rolls-Royce sale. The name did not last long, however, as customers were forever referring to his small but close team as 'those blokes in Lenham', so Kingsford-Booty reluctantly changed the firm's name to the Lenham Motor Company – which caused endless problems when, a few years later, the business relocated a few miles away to Harrietsham.

Away from hard tops, the firm became equally famous for its fastback conversions. In 1963, a customer commissioned the Lenham boys to produce an aluminium roof and Kamm tail-section for his Austin-Healey Sprite. Such was the response to its embryonic coachbuilding efforts, that the small concern was inundated with requests for replicas, the design being gradually refined until it bore little resemblance to the original car. But rolling aluminium proved overly time consuming, so Kingsford-Booty enrolled on a course to learn about glassfibre. Having made a plant pot, he felt well-versed enough to manufacture entire car bodies and, after a few false starts, Lenham

Lenham

The Triumph Spitfire also came in for a Lenham makeover.

went on to produce a tidy sideline in industrial mouldings through to the end of the '70s.

From the mid-'60s, the glassfibre Sprite/Midget makeover proved a major success once it was offered in DIY form, but it wasn't the easiest of conversions for the inexperienced. The donor car's entire tail end was removed, leaving just the doors and lip around each wheel arch. The door pillars were braced, and a new rear section was then grafted on. When the job was done properly, the result was an exceedingly attractive little GT, especially with the optional Le Mans bonnet which did much to disguise the car's origins.

Several well-known racing drivers cut their competition teeth in these diminutive sportsters, and the company offered lightweight panels for the racing crowd. The options list featured a modified A-series engine with a stage 3 cylinder head, Weber carburettor, free-flow exhaust and high-lift camshaft. A couple of cars were fitted with pushrod Ford power, and one was equipped with a heavily-tuned Lotus twin-cam unit. For those looking for a more civilised road car, Lenham also offered the conversion with a Targa roof from '66, for £158, the company stating in its promotional literature that this variant: 'Set a new standard of fashion as a smart town car.' But, though good looking, the lift-out lid didn't prove overly popular, finding few takers. Similarly, another project which did not achieve the popularity that it deserved, was the devilishly attractive GTO, an amalgam of Le Mans bonnet and new Ferrari

Lenham's GT raced proved briefly dominant in the late '60s national races.

The Darnval LM1 used the Lenham GT racer's chassis with Renault running gear.

Lenham's flirtation with F100 sports car racing was brief; the car proved uncompetitive.

206 Dino-like tail section to suit a Midget in open configuration. Around half-a-dozen GTOs were made by the factory.

The Lenham Motor Company was a hive of activity during this period, involved in numerous projects, not all of them profitable. A keen amateur competitor, Kingsford-Booty became embroiled in various motor racing activities throughout the '60s, at one point fielding no less than 15 Formula 3 cars all over Europe. The firm also flirted with building its own Formula Ford single-seaters under the Hamlen standard (Hamlen being an anagram of Lenham), the performance being thoroughly ordinary. But while these open-wheelers failed to rake in the plaudits, the Lenham sports-racers proved briefly dominant in national class GT racing.

Produced under the Lenham-Hurst Racing banner, by co-director and Formula 3 stalwart Roger Hurst, the first in a long line of increasingly outlandish Lenham sports-racers appeared in '68. The dramatic P79 coupé sported a semi-monocoque chassis with the choice of either Nerus-BMW or Cosworth FWA 'fours'. Although the P79 generally failed to live up to expectation, the following year's P80 development scooped the '69 STP series, in the hands of policeman and sometime works Rootes driver Ray Calcutt. The same model also lifted the '70 French GT championship spoils. Nine cars were built, including one with a 3-litre Repco-Brabham Formula 1 unit, which was briefly raced by Grand Prix back-marker Francois Migault. A smaller, open version, designed for the short-lived F100 series, proved uncompetitive and was immediately dropped from the line-up.

When the P79 was unveiled at the '69 Racing Cars Show, Kingsford-Booty was repeatedly asked if there was any likelihood of a road-going version. Three years later, a sparsely equipped car hit the streets with a box-section chassis, fully adjustable suspension, all-round disc brakes, a lift-up canopy in place of the previous gullwing door arrangement, and an integral rollcage. But the Lenham GT, as it was dubbed, proved so laborious to build that it sadly remained unique.

However, the GT did spawn an unlikely sports car project with a group of

Lenham Le Mans	
Made	Harrietsham, Kent
Engine	Front-mounted, water-cooled 1275cc ohv 'four'
Construction	Unitary steel with glassfibre outer skin
Top speed	110mph (dependent on spec)
0–60mph	10 seconds
Price new	£165 (conversion 1965)

French enthusiasts. The Darnval LM1 was conceived by Francis Lechere and Vincent Mausset as an inexpensive mid-engined GT. Kingsford-Booty and Peter Rix (who had joined Lenham in '70) took one of the sports-racer chassis and installed Renault R8 running gear, clothing it in a dramatic wedge-shaped glassfibre body. Kingsford-Booty spent a large portion of '72 helping to set up a manufacturing base in Ste Darnval, Le Havre, but the project collapsed the following year after just four cars had been completed. Plans to run Francois Migault in the Le Mans 24-hour race, in a race-modified example, died with it.

By way of a complete contrast, the early '70s saw one of Lenham's most profitable enterprises – the Arkley. Some years earlier, the firm had produced a glassfibre Austin-Healey replica body for John Britten's ModSports racer. A photographer and Morgan dealer, Britten had been searching for a profitable sideline to his business and, together with Kingsford-Booty, hatched this fun car. Unveiled at the '70 Racing Car Show, the Arkley swiftly became an extremely popular method of transforming the appearance of a moth-eaten Sprite or Midget, with very little outlay. The front and rear bodywork was removed from the donor car, and new glassfibre panels bonded on.

Though it appeared to have been dreamed up by Enid Blyton, the car was styled by Kingsford-Booty, who was later dismissive of his efforts, stating that: '(Britten) stood over me the whole time making "helpful" suggestions and altering things so it ended up looking like a Noddy car.' Even so, it was a huge sales success for John Britten Garages, Herefordshire, with Lenham producing the glassfibre panels. Early editions featured cut-away doors, although these were soon dropped in favour of standard Sprite/Midget units. In time, two models were offered, the S version featuring narrow wings for standard-size wheels, and the SS sporting chunky wheel arches to house wider rims. Although conceived as an inexpensive road car, several Arkleys took to the track, Gabriel Koenig and Britten himself finding considerable success in national club racing.

Lenham continued moulding Arkley panels for Britten until '87, when he sold the project rights to enthusiast Peter May, who carried on offering the conversion until '95, when the moulds were sold to a Stateside enthusiast. By this time, around 1200 kits had been supplied.

By the mid-'70s, the Lenham Motor Company had dramatically slowed down its car building operation. Roger Hurst set up on his own in '72, fielding all manner of single-seaters and sports cars (still under the Lenham-Hurst label), and running an indescribably ugly sports-prototype in the '76 Le Mans classic, before turning to supplying racing car components. Meanwhile, from '76 to '82, Kingsford-Booty and Rix turned their attentions to building an HWM-esque roadster based on an Austin-Healey frame, along with a four-seater MGB roadster conversion (one of Kingsford-Booty's favourite projects).

In the late-'80s, the firm reverted back to its original Vintage & Sports Car Garage status, concentrating on dealing in classic MGs and Triumphs. By this time, the moulds to Lenham's numerous designs were collecting dust. Ironically, when the rights to the name, along with assorted paraphernalia, were offered for sale in '98, the partners were inundated with requests for hard tops and Le Mans conversion, but it was the end of the road. The moulds and jigs moved on, and nothing more has been heard since.

The Arkley, here in SS trim, was one of a number of Lenham projects produced for outside firms.

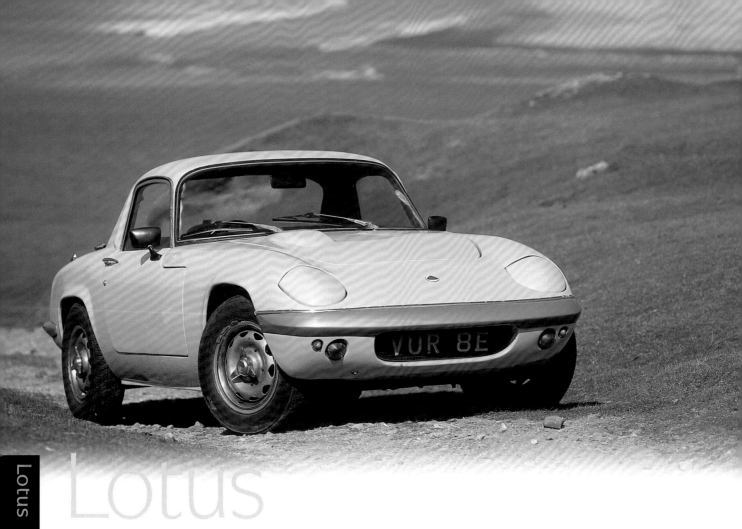

Lotus

The sublime Elan was launched in 1962 and was an instant success. Nearly 7500 examples were built.

The word 'genius' is bandied around with monotonous regularity but, in the annals of motor racing, no man deserved the tag more than Anthony Colin Bruce Chapman. A visionary, never afraid of experimentation, his creations scaled the heights of Formula One and the Indianapolis 500 while he enjoyed a parallel career as a motor mogul. But though he would latterly find fame for breaking moulds and pushing envelopes, his early efforts were rather more prosaic.

Chapman was studying engineering at University College, London when he constructed a trials car around the remains of an Austin Seven. Completed in 1948, the Lotus Mk1 proved successful but circuit racing remained the big draw, prompting him to join the 750 Motor Club, then a hot-bed of innovative thinking. The subsequent Lotus MkII used an Austin Seven chassis with 1172cc Ford sidevalve power. Demonstrating the originality that was to become a Chapman hallmark, in order to get the ideal axle ratio, he took the crownwheel from one ratio and a pinion from another, put the two in an axle full of grinding paste and ran it to match the gears roughly together. He then cleaned it out, fitted another set of bearings and installed it in the car. Though noisy, it worked.

The first truly racing-orientated Lotus, the MkIII, was put together with typical attention to detail, the desire being to keep weight down to the absolute minimum. With a healthy dollop of lateral thinking, Chapman divided the Austin engine's siamesed inlet ports, achieving a massive power gain. A second car was built with Ford power, followed by the MkIV, a one-off trials car.

During 1952, Chapman and cohort Michael Allen developed a new model with a view to series production as well as competition. Forsaking the Austin

Lotus Elan S4	
Made	Hethel, Norfolk
Engine	Front-mounted, water-cooled 1558cc twin-cam 'four'
Construction	Steel backbone chassis with glassfibre body
Top speed	120mph
0–60mph	7.5 seconds
Price new	£1486 (1970)

chassis, the MkVI boasted a lightweight spaceframe incorporating stressed floor and side panels to maximise strength and minimise weight. The bare chassis weighed just 55lbs. Clothed in an aluminium skin by famed panel beaters Williams & Pritchard, this new model was sold in kit form leaving the builder to source most of the componentry. The first example was fitted with a Ford Consul 1500cc motor and was race ready by July 1952. Offered with the choice of Ford sidevalve, Consul or MG TD power, the car had its front end suspended by a Ford beam axle split and pivoted to make it independent, while the Ford 10 rear axle was located by a Panhard rod and sprung by telescopic dampers. By the end of the year, the model was selling in enough numbers for Chapman to quit his day job and form Lotus Engineering.

The MkVI was well received by the press, *Autocar* commenting: 'A run in a Ford 10-powered Lotus showed the handling qualities of the car are of a very high order indeed. There can be few cars, if any, which are quicker through S-bends.' With a mildly tuned sidevalve engine, Lotus claimed a top speed of 93mph and 45mpg. During a three-year production run to 1955, some 100 cars were built.

But it was in 1957 that the embryonic firm reached maturity with two new road cars – the immortal Seven and the technologically advanced Elite. The former was effectively an evolution of the MkVI. However, though outwardly similar, a number of changes were made beneath the skin. While the MkVI had used a spaceframe with larger-section bottom twin rails, the Seven's sported thinner-diameter rails, with the centre section, transmission tunnel and axle mounts from the XI sports-racer.

Though the prototype used a de Dion rear end, production cars featured the improbable Austin-Nash Metropolitan live rear axle located by trailing arms and coil springs. The front end was suspended by twin wishbones aping the XI's arrangement with an anti-roll bar plus coil springs. Predictably, the venerable 1172cc Ford sidevalve 'four' provided propulsion although if 40bhp wasn't enough, Lotus offered the Super Seven from December '58 with a 75bhp Coventry Climax engine. Capable of over 100mph and 0–60mph in just 9.2 seconds, the Super Seven cost £120 more than the regular item (£536 as a kit, £1036 fully built).

The following year saw the arrival of the Lotus Seven A with a 948cc BMC A-series engine which, though producing only 37bhp (three less than the Ford lump), was infinitely more tuneable. This variation on the theme also spawned the Seven America which used the slightly more powerful Austin-Healey Sprite A-series, Stateside editions identifiable by their 'clamshell' wings in place of cycle mudguards.

Peter Gammons, seen here with his MkVI, was one of Lotus's leading protagonists in the mid-'50s.

Lotus

The immortal Lotus Seven redefined the word basic, yet became an automotive icon.

Though Chapman was latterly dismissive of the Seven, claiming that it was: 'The sort of thing that could be dashed off in a weekend', the car's popularity has endured to this day and, for a small period during the late-'50s, it was Lotus's only production model.

And that was because the simply gorgeous Elite was proving such a nightmare to productionise. Chapman freely admitted that he was never all that interested in road cars but the Elite was needed as a revenue earner for his nascent Grand Prix team – ironic then, that he should lose money on all 1050 or so cars made. And it isn't especially difficult to understand why.

Keen to minimise the use of steel in the Elite's construction, Chapman and his team decided to design the world's first glassfibre monocoque (sort of). Structurally, the car was composed of three major mouldings, deriving its strength from eight box-sections. At the rear, a triangular box provided attachment points for the suspension, while the propshaft tunnel, sills and roof acted as stressed sections. The only metalwork in the entire structure was a steel hoop joining the roof, scuttle and sills, plus a sheet steel bar below the windscreen to support the steering column and handbrake.

But if the car's construction raised more than a few eyebrows, the styling captivated seemingly everyone. Penned by accountant Peter Kirwan-Taylor (his irregular body of work also including the lamentable Citroën Bijou) with input from Chapman, the Elite was breathtakingly beautiful. It was also extremely

This is how the customer received the complete Seven package.

slippery with a drag coefficient of an amazing 0.29 thanks to some fettling by aerodynamicist Frank Costin. Inside it was equally swish with vinyl-clad, Dunlop-made seats and an attractive dashboard designed by Peter Cambridge.

Predictably, Chapman had high expectations of the diminutive coupé's power-to-weight ratio, which were never likely to be realised after opting for the flyweight Coventry Climax FWA four-pot using the block and bore of its FWB sister. Even so, despite its tiny capacity of just 1216cc, the newly christened FEW produced from 75bhp to as much as 110bhp.

Initial problems with laying up the complex glassfibre mouldings caused manufacturing delays, as did the lack of factory space, Chapman eventually taking up the option of land in Cheshunt on which to construct a new, purpose-built facility. A steady trickle of cars soon reached their expectant owners but it was not until late-'59 that production rose to 15, then 20 cars per week.

Though originally envisaged as a pure road car, it came as no surprise that many Elites found their way trackside. Ian Walker was the first to campaign his example, winning on the car's debut at a May '58 Silverstone meeting. The following year saw the private entry of Lumsden/Riley finish an astonishing eighth overall in the Le Mans 24-hour classic, notching up the first of six straight class victories at La Sarthe for the Elite.

Improvements followed for the lightly reworked Series 2 model in 1960, this year also seeing the arrival of the Special Equipment edition with larger carburettors and tuned exhaust. But the end was nigh as the Elite became simply too expensive to produce, the model being dropped from the line-up in 1963.

But for all the Elite's headline grabbing, the Seven was still selling moderately well. In an effort to make it cheaper to produce in volume, the series 2 variant of 1960 featured glassfibre wings and a glassfibre nose cone

The sublime Lotus Elite had a class-leading drag coefficient of just 0.29.

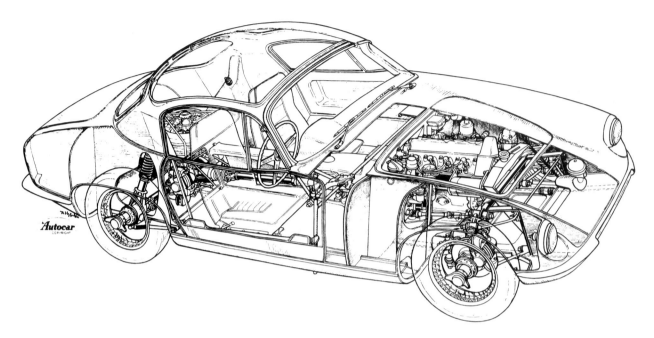

This cutaway view of an Elite shows the glassfibre 'monocoque' construction.

designed by John Frayling. The other obvious visual change was the adoption of 15-inch wheels in place of the previous 13-inch versions. The same choice of powerplants remained, but with the option of a Ford pre-crossflow Anglia 105E unit which became standard fitment in October of that year, the A-series lump being dropped for good. The Super Seven meanwhile featured a 95bhp Cosworth-tuned 1498cc Ford Cortina 'four', with front disc brakes from a Triumph Spitfire. Sevens were by now manufactured under the Lotus Components banner.

But if Chapman had had his way, the Seven would have been killed off some years earlier. Originally conceived as a replacement for the rudimentary roadster, the sublime Elan launched at the October '62 Earls Court Motor Show swiftly became a more 'grown-up' proposition. Learning from mistakes made with the Elite, this dainty little sportster featured a backbone-chassis weighing a mere 75lbs with crossmembers and turrets at the front cradling the engine.

And what an engine. First seen in the back of the Lotus 23 sports-racer, this twin-cam 'four' was based on a Ford Cortina block with a Harry Mundy (formally of BRM) designed DOHC alloy cylinder head. Though it originally displaced 1499cc, all 22 examples made with this displacement were later

Les Leston's DAD10 takes the inside line on Graham Warner's LOV1, the two most famous examples of the Elite model.

The diminutive Elan was another Lotus landmark, seen here in Series 1 trim.

revised to the definitive 1558cc configuration for fear of customers over-revving the delicate jewel-like motor. Transmission was a Ford Classic four-speeder, front suspension consisting of pressed steel wishbones with coil springs, the rear end using a wide lower wishbone and coils arrangement. Inside, the well-appointed sports car featured adjustable seats, and a wooden dash' fronted by an adjustable steering wheel.

Offered in component form for £1095 or fully built at £1495, the Elan proved an instant success, but build quality was still an alien concept at Lotus. Early criticisms centred around the rubber suspension doughnuts which twisted into knots, and the cabin furniture that fell easily to hand before falling off. Even so, over 2000 cars had been sold before many of the problems were addressed by the Elan S2 launched in November '64. Improvements included a walnut dashboard in place of the previous nine-ply teak affair, new tail-light clusters, quick-release filler cap, larger front calipers, plus various suspension tweaks. Before the S2 bowed out in June '66, the last batch boasted the Special Equipment package that consisted of a 115bhp engine, close-ratio 'box, centre-lock wheels (previously an option) and indicators down on the flanks.

But for all the Elan's sales success, there were still a number of potential customers put off by the car's lack of a lid. Lotus responded in September with the S3 edition. Aside from the fixed-head coupé roof, other exterior changes included an extended boot with the lock located above the number plate, while inside there were new nylon carpets and a plusher level of trim. Offered at £1596, it proved instantly popular. Following the demise of the S2, Lotus introduced an open version of the S3 from June '66, featuring electric windows in fixed-frames and subtly altered doors.

That same year also saw the introduction of Chapman's 'Car for Europe' – the sublime if slightly quirky Europa, Lotus's first mid-engined road car. It wasn't the first production car to have its engine centrally mounted – René Bonnet, De Tomaso and ATS got there first – but none was particularly affordable or met with even a modicum of success on the showroom floor. But Chapman's new baby undoubtedly did.

The Elan +2 marked Lotus's move to provide a sports car for the family man.

The Seven S4 was vilified by purists for its 'soft' character, but proved the most successful Lotus-built Seven.

Based on an Elan-derived backbone chassis with a Y-frame at the rear to house the engine, there was nothing overly exotic about the car's construction. Front suspension was a double-wishbone arrangement lifted virtually untouched from the Triumph Spitfire with GT6 front hubs. The Triumph parts bin also supplied the (Lotus-modified) steering column. The rear end used meaty radius arms pivoted on the chassis where the 'Y' separated. The steel wheels, similar in appearance to the Elan's, hid disc brakes at the front, drums at the back.

If the chassis and suspension set-up were proven commodities, the choice of powerplant caused a few raised eyebrows. In search of an engine with an integral transaxle, Chapman hopped over the channel to Renault. The Regie's all-alloy 1.5-litre 'four' from the innovative R16 hatchback was mounted amidships and reversed to transmit drive to the rear wheels. Power output was also upped to 78bhp thanks to a higher compression ratio, larger valves and a twin-choke Solex carburettor.

Even more controversial than the choice of motor was the car's 'bread van' styling. Penned by Lotus stalwart John Frayling, the Europa was remarkably aerodynamic (cd 0.29), but the deft touch that marked the Elite as an instant classic, and the Elan's subtle delicacy of line, were noticeably absent.

Because of the double curvature of the side windows, they were fixed in place. Ventilation was totally inadequate, air forced into the cabin by Renault nozzles mounted in the wooden dash'. The cloying confines of the Europa's cabin could prove intolerable over long distances and were particularly unappealing for claustrophobics. But the Europa was fast. Despite its piddling powerplant, the featherweight machine could top 115mph, but the chassis could patently handle more horses. Unveiled to the press in December '66, production commenced the following year, the first 500 cars destined for Lotus's French dealerships.

In 1968, the venerable Seven was given a new lease of life thanks to the insertion of a new 85bhp, 1.6-litre Ford Cortina motor for the Series 3 edition. Other changes included a Ford Escort Mexico rear axle in place of the prehistoric Standard unit, while inside there were a few token concessions to civility – for the first time you got a fuel gauge and indicators!

If that wasn't enough, Lotus introduced the Seven S at the '69 Racing Car Show complete with a 120bhp Holbay-tuned engine that could reach 60mph in 7.4 seconds on the way to an aerodynamically-blunted 107mph top end. Later that year, there was also the option of a Lotus twin-cam-powered Seven; the SS. For years, owners had begged the factory to produce a Seven with this engine, but Lotus's back room boffins insisted that it wouldn't fit. One customer proved them wrong, and, with the assistance of Graham Nearn of Caterham Cars who had taken the sole concession for the endearing roadster in '67, the Holbay-modded twin-cam SS became an official model. But not for long, as just 13 of these machines were built.

For all the Seven's enduring popularity, Colin Chapman became increasingly embarrassed by the stark roadster. As he became older, he insisted that he produced cars that he wanted to drive, hence the Elan +2 launched in 1967. Though an evolution of the Elan theme, it was a very different, softer sports car. Intended as a civilised, more upmarket variant, the +2 boasted an extremely stylish glassfibre body styled by Ron Hickman, derived from a stillborn prototype dubbed the Metier.

Underneath the graceful silhouette sat a regular Elan backbone stretched by

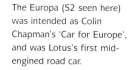

The Europa (S2 seen here) was intended as Colin Chapman's 'Car for Europe', and was Lotus's first mid-engined road car.

The Europa's cabin was not ideal for anyone above 5ft 8in tall, and could prove uncomfortable over long distances.

23 inches with a seven-inch wider track. Suspension was virtually identical despite the 315lb increase in weight. Powering the newcomer was the same 118bhp 'twink' from its smaller sibling, which meant it lagged behind in performance notwithstanding the more streamlined shape. Top speed was around 120mph, the 0–60mph dash taking a whisker over eight seconds.

Inside, this was Lotus's most luxurious effort yet, with a shiny mahogany fascia, two-waveband radio, and seats that tipped forward for access to the two occasional rear seats. With an introduction price of £1672 in component form or £1923 ready-made, the +2 was an instant success and was joined by the plusher-still +2S the following year. This variant had the distinction of being the first Lotus road car not offered in DIY form.

March '68 saw a further evolution of the regular Elan, the S4 featuring squared-off wheel arches to accommodate fatter tyres, larger tail-light clusters, bonnet bulge to clear the new twin-choke Webers (from November that year), and a reworked dashboard. The Europa meanwhile received minor improvements for the coming of the Series 2, of most benefit to future restorers being the adoption of a separate body-chassis assembly in place of the bonded-on arrangement of the S1. Another welcome addition was the move to opening windows, or rather sliding glass that did at least make cabin-heat dissipation that much easier. Initially offered for export markets only, Lotus offered the car for UK consumption from July '69 for £1667 factory-built.

Three months earlier, Colin Chapman had given Mike Warner, Chief Executive of Lotus Components, £5000 and a free hand to devise an all-new Seven for the '70s. The existing model was considered an embarrassment and a loss maker. The Series 4 edition needed to be cheaper to build and would be sold through a new dealer network, aimed at the Spitfire/MG Midget market. Seven months later, the fruit of Warner's labours was shown to the boss.

Styled by Alan Barrett, the latest take on the Seven theme was visually far removed from its forerunners. Longer and wider, the S4 eschewed aluminium for colour-impregnated glassfibre. The rear wings, scuttle and dashboard were integral, the dramatically swooping front wings and flip-forward bonnet separate panels. Mechanically, the Ford Escort rear axle remained in place but was located by a Watt's linkage, the front suspension aping that of the Europa. Engine options ranged from 1.3-litre Ford to Lotus twin-cam, with the Corsair gearbox replacing the previous Cortina unit. And if the purists railed against the car's soft image, they were given ample ammunition by the uncommonly civilised cabin that, aside from being discernibly more spacious, even featured an ashtray.

Making its public debut at the '70 Geneva Salon, the S4 prompted a mixed reaction. Some cited it as being a Tupperware Seven cum beach buggy pastiche; others loved its bold lines. And it was to prove the best-selling Lotus Seven, with up to 15 cars finding homes each week. But it continued to sit uneasily in the firm's model line-up. Chapman was keen to push Lotus's image up-market, so the Seven had to go. In October '72, the last example left the factory after around 600 had been made, the rights to the model passing to Caterham Cars the following year.

Similarly, the venerable Elan's days were almost numbered. Announced in October '70, the S4 Sprint featured a 'Big-Valve' twin-cam developed by Tony Rudd, so-called because of its improved alloy cylinder head with larger inlet valves. A higher compression ratio and Dell'Orto carbs (later changed to Webers) helped push output to 126bhp at 6500rpm, the very last cars featuring five-speed 'boxes. Offered in a variety of two-tone paint schemes with large stripes down the flank bearing the legend 'Sprint', this little roadster could reach 60mph in a claimed 5.9 seconds, but production was over by August '73. Around 8000 Elans of all types had been built.

Likewise, the +2 was facing the chop as the new breed of Elite and Esprit models were in the pipeline. In February '71, the 2S had been replaced with the +2S 130, featuring the 'Big-Valve' engine, this latest variant identifiable by its self-coloured silver roof. From October '72, a five-speed Lotus 'box (with Austin Maxi internals) was offered in the +2S 130/5, but it was the end of the road by '74 after around 5200 of these delectable coupés had been sold.

Amazingly, the Europa continued to rack up sales into the mid-'70s. And in 1971 it had received the power boost its chassis had been crying out for, thanks to the insertion of Lotus's twin-cam 'four'. The Europa Twin-Cam was identifiable by its cropped rear fins, cut down to the level of the rear deck. That, and the attractive 'Spider' alloy-wheels. Capable of 120mph and 0–60mph in 7.5 seconds, it was just a precursor to the Special introduced towards the end of '72. Featuring the 'Big-Valve' engine allied to Renault's latest 16TX five-speeder, it could top 125mph, most customers requesting the charismatic black and gold colour scheme associated with Lotus's John Player Special-sponsored Grand Prix winners. But by 1975, the Europa was forced to make way for the Esprit by which time around 9230 Europas of all types had been made.

That Lotus has survived more than 50 years is a testimony to the design integrity of its cars, if not perhaps, the build quality. Chapman died in December '82 but his legacy is a series of individualistic sporting chariots revered the world over.

The Europa Twin-Cam was identifiable by its cropped rear fins.

Marcos

The 3-litre Ford V6-powered Marcos was launched at the '69 London Racing Car Show, and proved an instant hit.

Marcos 1800	
Made	Bradford-on-Avon, Wiltshire
Engine	Front-mounted, water-cooled 1780cc ohv 'four'
Construction	Wooden platform with glassfibre body
Top Speed	124mph
0–60mph	8.3 seconds
Price new	£1885

If ever there was an automotive marque that has led a chequered existence, it's Marcos. Umpteen times it has foundered on the rocks of calamity, only to wash up on the shore of prosperity as the tide changes. And its survival is largely down to the pugilistic savvy of one Jeremy George Weston Marsh, former stuntman and instigator of the marque.

The saga of Marsh and his extraordinary cars dates back to 1955. On leaving the navy, the young Westcountryman found work with Dante Engineering, who produced tuning equipment for Austin Sevens. Concluding that he could do a better job himself, he quickly left to form Speedex Castings & Accessories, offering a similar service from premises in Luton, Bedfordshire. Within two years, Marsh had established himself as the country's leading purveyor of Austin performance parts as diverse as demon cylinder heads, alloy wheels, and a trick independent front suspension conversion using a transverse leaf spring and wishbone at the bottom. He also added a tidy sideline in alloy and glassfibre bodyshells, offering just about anything the budding specials builder desired.

A fearless driver himself, Marsh gained fame for his efforts in the 750 Motor Club's various racing formulae that spawned the likes of Colin Chapman and Eric Broadley. And it was through this organisation that he came into contact with aerodynamicist and former Olympic swimmer, Frank Costin. Marsh, universally known as Jem, was intrigued by Irishman Costin's lyrical waxings about the virtues of wood in car construction, pointing out that if it worked for aeroplanes such as the Mosquito, it would be good enough for something as prosaic as a racing car.

In the spring of '59 the pair hatched a plan to build an ultra-lightweight clubmans car in the Lotus Seven idiom but constructed of wood and with full weather protection. Costin would be responsible for the car's Mosquito-style plywood monocoque, with Marsh taking care of the running gear. There followed the formation of the Monocoque Body Chassis Company Ltd to build the car in Dolgellau, North Wales, Mrs Costin's home town. The firm set up shop in a dingy converted coach house behind the town's Lion Hotel. Costin initially worked alone but, by the end of the year, it became clear that more help was required. Dennis Adams had previously worked with Costin at Lister building chassis, and in December '59 joined the team, his carpenter brother Peter following suit not long after.

Early the following year, the prototype was finished. Dubbed the Marcos (MARsh-COStin) by Costin's father in law, it sported a rigid structure comprising three torsional boxes running fore-and-aft and three cross-ways. The two side boxes were of triangular section facing downwards, while the central box enclosed the propshaft. Powering the machine was a tuned 1172cc Ford sidevalve 'four', the Austin A40 rear axle located by trailing arms and a Panhard rod, the front end suspended by Costin-fabricated wishbones.

Aesthetically, the Marcos was grotesquely proportioned, but it was fast and sleek, topping 110mph. The first customer car was completed in May '60 with a Cosworth-tuned Ford 105E unit and, by August, a new fully enveloped nose that would become standard equipment for future cars. Owner and former ERA driver Bill Moss started ten races that year, winning nine of them. Predictably, the racing fraternity was quick to embrace the Marcos and, by November of that year, Marsh had received orders for six cars. One went to wealthy enthusiast Barry Filer who installed unknown racer Jackie Stewart as his designated driver.

By the time that these orders had been fulfilled, it was becoming increasingly obvious that new premises were not only desirable, but essential. With the help of the Welsh Industry Board, a suitable manufacturing facility was found at the former RAF base at Llanberis. Unfortunately, negotiations dragged on interminably so the Caernarvonshire County Council arranged to install the fledgling firm in the former dining hall of Brynrefail Grammar School as a temporary measure.

After the eighth chassis had been completed, Dennis Adams left to work with Marsh in Luton, leaving brother Peter to head the production team, now five strong. Costin meanwhile had become increasingly distracted by non-Marcos projects, and was at odds with Marsh about the company's future direction. The two split in early '61, Marsh travelling to Wales to recover all the jigs and then entrusting them to the Adams brothers. They then set up

The very first Frank Costin-designed Marcos wasn't aesthetically pleasing.

shop in Speedex's Luton workshop, Dennis Adams giving the car a makeover with faired-in front lights and lower roofline while still retaining the distinctive gullwing doors. The restyled Marcos still wasn't ravishing, but proved a vast improvement over Costin's original.

But the Adams boys were convinced that the future lay with an all-new body, concocting a more cohesive shape with many of the

Chris McLaren campaigning one of the fabled 'Ugly Duckling' Marcos GTs.

non-stressed body panels made of glassfibre. The first of these new Marcos GTs was delivered in April '61 to future Lotus F1 driver Jackie Oliver who promptly crashed it. The second was retained by the company and entered in that year's Le Mans 24-hour race where it retired with engine problems. Offered in kit form with Ford Anglia 105E power for £830, these 'Luton Gullwings' continued to sell well throughout the year, but Marsh ran into financial difficulties. Interest in specials building was starting to ebb and Speedex was suffering as a result, the sister Monocoque Chassis & Body Co concern proving a drain on reserves.

Dennis and Peter Adams returned to their home village of Great Shelford, near Cambridge, to concentrate on their own design projects while Marsh searched for a financial saviour. In a corrugated shed, the brothers conceived two new machines. The first was an open-top variation of the 'Gullwing' GT, but the main project of '62 was the extraordinary XP supercar. This design featured a rear-mounted Chevrolet flat-six engine, three abreast seating with central steering (pre-dating the McLaren F1 by three decades), plus ground-effect aerodynamics.

Meanwhile, Jem Marsh finalised discussions with retired naval officer Greville Cavendish, with whom he persuaded the Adams brothers to meet in October '62. A deal was struck whereby Cavendish would pay off any debts, and would finance the resumption of car manufacture while developing the XP as a Marcos along with the open version of the 'Gullwing' car.

From new premises in Bradford-on-Avon, the newly formed Marcos Cars Ltd revived production of the Adams-restyled 'Gullwing'. Marsh realised that as long as the firm was perceived solely as a manufacturer of racing cars, output was always going to be limited. So the XP would be the firm's priority, while the following January the Spyder variant was displayed at the Racing Car Show. Against expectations, orders were hard to come by, as it was too basic to be a proper road car while the racing crowd demanded a fixed lid for competition. So the Spyder remained unique, a fastback variant offered from mid-'63. This 'bread van'-like affair was cobbled together by dropping a vast slab of polystyrene on top of the car before hacking at it with knives until it looked 'about right'. A mould was taken, and the roof was offered as an option but found only two takers – others had the roof permanently bonded on.

With sales of racing cars being largely seasonal and the XP some way off completion, Marsh instructed the Adams brothers to come up with a stop-gap to bring in some much-needed revenue. The Costin principles of wooden construction were retained but this new design was to be a pure road car and largely designed around Marsh's 6ft 4in frame. After Marcos improbably toyed with the idea of building its own engine, the unlikely Volvo B18 straight-four unit was chosen, the resultant prototype displayed at the '64 Racing Car Show. It caused a sensation, press and public alike clamouring to get a closer look at the exotic-looking Marcos 1800.

And it isn't difficult to understand why. With its impossibly long, priapic nose, and aggressive, kicked-up rear haunches, this new machine looked for all the world like it had stepped out of some Latin *carrozzeria*. Exuberant rather than extravagant, the car's styling was truly original and free of the unnecessary addenda that were to blight the perfectly realised silhouette in the decades to come. The 1800 swiftly became the chariot of choice for the 'beautiful people'. Prince Albrecht of Liechtenstein placed an order, as did Lord Lilford and Lord Cross. But, for all the media hype and product placement (one car featured prominently in *The Saint* among other TV shows), sales proved disappointingly sluggish. Part of the problem lay in the £1500 price tag. In a bid to make the car more affordable, the expensive de Dion independent rear suspension arrangement was dropped after the first 33 cars had been built, replaced by a Ford live axle. This afforded a reduction in price to £1340 but with little corresponding increase in sales.

Marsh had, however, found a tidy revenue earner in the (mis)shape of the Mini Marcos. The notion of this irredeemably ugly yet strangely endearing little coupé was born of a meeting with test pilot Dizzy Addicott at the '63 Racing Car Show. A keen amateur racing driver in machines such as a Buick small-block V8-equipped Lotus 15, Addicott had constructed a special around the innards of a Mini van. Dubbed the DART (Dizzy Addicott Racing Team), this aluminium-bodied machine wasn't exactly a vision of loveliness but Marsh felt it had potential to be a money-spinner.

Addicott commissioned Falcon Shells, a firm in which Greville Cavendish had a financial stake, to build glassfibre 'shells for production cars. Marsh disagreed with the DART's creator on the perceived target audience. Believing that its future lay with the cheap 'n' cheerful end of the market rather than the discerning automotive connoisseur Addicott was keen to attract, Marsh collaborated with Malcolm Newell on a redesigned and vastly simplified version. Former AC man Newell, who would later find fame for his award-

The Denis Adams-styled Marcos spider proved a non-starter; all were ordered with fastback roofs.

Marcos transformed its image with the sensational 1800, finding a number of high-profile customers.

winning Quasar motorcycle, was instructed to produce a monocoque body/chassis unit into which Mini parts could be incorporated with modification. This cost-conscious design process extended to the use of the donor car's radiator which necessitated the elevated bonnet line that continues to come in for criticism from anyone with aesthetic sensibilities. But this insistence on using every last widget from the Mini proved a masterstroke, as when announced in *Motor Sport* in late-'65, it had a launch price of just £199. From that one advertisement, there were 144 enquiries about the Mini Marcos.

It wasn't long before the racing crowd took more than a passing interest in the diminutive sportster. A French-owned car was entered for the '66 Le Mans round-the-clock classic driven by Jean-Louis Marnat and future European GT champion and NASCAR back-marker Claude Ballot-Lena. With a 1275cc Cooper 'S'-spec engine prepared by BMC's Special Tuning department, the car was blisteringly fast but appeared to be held together with duck tape and bailing twine. Jem Marsh paid a visit to La Sarthe to watch its progress and spent most of his stay apologising for the car's appearance, convinced that it would retire within minutes of the start. But the baby Marcos completed 2152 miles at an average speed of nearly 90mph, lifting the *Motor* trophy for first (and in this instance only) British car to cross the line. An odd twist to the story was the news that the car was stolen almost immediately after the race. Some less charitable among the race entrants were convinced that it only 'disappeared' because the team knew that it would fail the post-event scrutineering.

For all the scurrilous rumours, the Mini Marcos's success in the most publicised race in the world assured the car's future. Marsh could barely keep up with demand. However, this wasn't the case with its 1800 big brother. For all its undoubted good looks and success on the track (one example won the hard-fought Freddie Dixon Memorial series driven by Chris Boulter), it seemed that Marsh couldn't give the cars away. The situation reached crisis point when 1800s were being stockpiled. In a bid to reduce production costs, giving a lower selling price, the Volvo engine was replaced by a 1.5-litre Ford unit for 1966. Around 106 of the 'Swedish cars' had been built in two years.

But there lingered a perceived stigma to Ford products and Marsh was quick in replacing the blue oval's rocker covers with Marcos's own in an effort to disguise the engine's origins, the Weber carburettor being ditched in favour of twin Strombergs. He needn't have worried as Ford's 'Total Performance' programme was in full force, with GT40s making in-roads to greatness in sports car racing, and Lotus Cortinas dominating in tin-top events. The Ford badge now equalled competition pedigree, and the switch to the new engine saw the Marcos sales graph near vertical. To capitalise on the new-found prosperity, Marsh entered an agreement with Lawrencetune for an over-bored 1650cc edition, company principal Chris Lawrence boosting output from 85bhp to 120bhp. Some 32 cars were so-equipped in '67, by which time the option was dropped as Ford's new 1599cc crossflow superseded the 1.5 litre unit.

That same year Lawrence joined forces with Marsh for a crack at Le Mans with a works-prepared Mini Marcos. Despite being forced to make umpteen changes to the car to appease overzealous scrutineers (including raising the windscreen height by two centimetres which scrubbed 3mph off the top speed thanks to raising the car's drag coefficient) the duo were competitive in class until the transfer gears failed four hours into the race.

By the following year, Marcos Cars was immersed in myriad projects including a stillborn Mini-based hatchback for the Israeli Autocars concern, and a two-pronged attack on Le Mans. A 2-litre B20 Volvo-powered coupé was entered, along with a brand new design; the XP Mantis. Neither was to make the race. While the modified production car proved too slow to make the grid, the bespoke sports-racer never even made it as far as France.

A mid-engined prototype built to meet the FIA's Group 6, 3-litre GT regulations, the XP was another Dennis Adams-penned project and bore his trademark stylistic flamboyance. A wedge-shaped device with Repco-Brabham V8 power, this extraordinary racer employed a stressed-plywood monocoque, the radiators set either side of the cockpit much like contemporary Matras, with double-curvature doors and clear Perspex roof and rear bonnet section. Adams was never altogether happy with the car's appearance. His original design called for a one-piece canopy that could be opened either side, but simple piano hinges were used on the leading edges of the windows. The car made only one 'competitive' outing, at the '68 Spa-Francorchamps 1000-kilometre race where Marsh shared with Eddie Nelson. In treacherous conditions, the XP was lying well down the order when water got into the alternator following a spin. A chronic misfire set in, and the car was withdrawn for fear of grenading the engine.

The Mini Marcos sold in four figures despite its controversial looks.

Marcos

Marcos bodyshells awaiting finishing on the production line at Westbury in 1970.

Following its Belgian adventure, a Buick V8 lump was installed, Marsh using the XP as his road car. But there were to be no more trackside forays for a while, as the Marcos factory was flooded after the River Avon burst its banks. The Mantis racer was sold to a US enthusiast as efforts were made to get road car production back underway. But the disappointment of failing to qualify the coupé at Le Mans rankled Marsh, and he promised himself that nobody would ever accuse a Marcos of being underpowered again, hence the launch of a 3-litre Ford V6-equipped version at the '69 London Racing Car Show. This 144bhp machine proved an instant hit, early customers including Rod Stewart, TV presenter John Noakes, and movie auteur Sam Wanamaker. Another, more obscure patron was S.B. Knudsen, then president of the Ford Motor Company.

The final year of the '60s also marked the end of the road for the wooden chassis. Despite having proved its strength and durability through racing, potential punters remained unconvinced about the material, necessitating the switch to an Adams brothers'-designed steel affair. The net result of the change was a 15-hour reduction in build time and significant cost saving. Around this time, Marsh also returned to Volvo power, primarily for the American market where the Ford unit flunked emission control tests.

92

Unfortunately, the Swedish straight-six was considerably heavier than the blue oval lump, causing an adverse effect on the car's deft handling.

These developments coincided with the move to a new, larger factory in Westbury, primarily to cope with Stateside-demand. Marcos continued to experiment with other engine options, Triumph's silky smooth 2.5-litre straight-six was fitted to 11 cars, Ford's thrashy Corsair V4 to a further handful. But, as if that was not enough, the firm also found time to develop an all-new car in time for the '69 Earls Court Motor Show. The radical Mantis bore little resemblance to the ill-starred, similarly monikered sports-racer of the previous year. A controversial design, Marcos's wonder wedge was a full four-seater with fuel-injected 2498cc Triumph power (the prototype being fitted with a Ford V6). Dennis Adams latterly attempted to distance himself from the project, claiming that his original renderings were vastly altered. Even so, 32 were made by mid-'71 when Marcos Cars effectively died – for the first time at least.

The move to the new manufacturing facility caused major disruptions in productivity. The second blow occurred when 27 cars were impounded by US Customs in the belief that they didn't meet the country's emission laws (they did), which caused the American distributor to go to the wall. Marcos was left facing financial ruin and the only option left to Marsh was to sell out to Hebron & Medlock Bath Engineering. But after just sixth months' trading, the company called in the receivers, selling off Marcos assets to cover its debts. The Rob Walker Group bought the factory only to hold a closing-down sale for the remaining bodyshells and chassis. Marcos was no more.

Unbowed, Marsh set up a spares and restoration facility next door to Walker's premises, while continuing to churn out Mini Marcoses until '76 (latterly with hatchbacks) when the rights passed to D&H Techniques of Lancashire. That same year, he bought back the Marcos moulds and jigs, reviving the marque in '81. Since then, the firm has endured umpteen ups and downs, even managing a return to Le Mans in '95, but at the time of writing, its future once more hangs in the balance.

The controversial four-seater Marcos Mantis was unfairly blamed for the collapse of the firm.

Ogle

The fabulous Ogle Triplex GTS was briefly owned by Prince Philip who sold it on after feeling 'decidedly conspicuous'.

David Ogle was a romantic. He dreamed of taking on the Italian car styling clique at their own game, but fate intervened just as he began to realise this vision. Ogle was a talented industrial designer, and had made a name for himself penning radios and TV sets for Bush, before taking his first tentative steps into the coachbuilding arena in 1960 with the Ogle 1.5. Trumpeted as a 'New conception of the business executive's personal car', this amorphous, glassfibre-bodied coupé came with a hefty £1574 price tag.

Underneath the car's distinctive silhouette was nothing more exotic than a Riley 1.5 floorpan, so you *really* had to want one. Only the lateral and longitudinal chassis rails from the donor car were retained, with additional steel tube reinforcement at key stress points. Front suspension was the unmodified Riley independent torsion bar set-up, and the rear axle was suspended on coil springs, and located by twin radius arms and an A-frame. Power came from a 68bhp, 1489cc 'four', giving a top speed of around 90mph. For all its virtues, only eight examples of the car were sold by the time the project was quietly dropped in mid-'62.

As the 1.5 was phased out, Ogle Design launched its take on the Mini. Dubbed the SX1000, it shared several styling elements with its forerunner, in particular the gracefully arced window line and minimal rear overhang. Initially, BMC was reluctant to supply componentry to the small Hertfordshire concern. Typically, customers would supply a new Mini along with a cheque for £550. In return, they would receive a lavishly equipped, baby GT.

Ultimately, BMC relented and agreed to supply parts on the proviso that no mention of the word Mini featured in the firm's publicity material. Potential

Ogle SX1000	
Made	Letchworth, Hertfordshire
Engine	Front-mounted, water-cooled 998cc ohv 'four'
Construction	Steel platform with glassfibre body
Top speed	101mph
0–60mph	11 seconds
Price new	£1085 (1962)

94

The Ogle 1.5 used Riley componentry. The high price blunted sales, with just eight cars finding homes.

The lovely Ogle SX1000 was arguably the best of the '60s Mini-based specialist sports cars.

punters now had the desirable option of a Cooper-spec 997cc A-series engine, giving a top end of 95mph. For the motor sport fraternity, the firm also offered the Lightweight GT, with thinner glassfibre panelling and a built-in roll-cage. Company director Sir John Whitmore – later to become European Saloon Car Champion driving a Lotus-Cortina – sprinted the sole example made, with some success. It was in this machine that David Ogle lost his life in '62, after crashing into a lorry following a visit to Brands Hatch.

The company was already facing financial ruin. While the industrial design arm was profitable, Ogle lost around £300 on each SX1000 built. Production was gradually wound up, the final stragglers leaving the factory in late-'64. Just 66 cars had been built. Without a full-time leader to keep things afloat, chairman John Ogier hired Czechoslovakian-born stylist Tom Karen to run the company until a suitable replacement could be found.

A former winner of the prestigious Institute of British Carriage and Automobile Manufacturers design award, Karen was given six months in which to prove himself (four decades on and he is still there). His main priority was to complete a contract with Bush, but Ogle was also committed to building a batch of bespoke Daimler SP250s for the boss of the Helena Rubinstein cosmetics group. Karen inherited the project at the clay modelling stage in May '62, and a car was required to be on display at the Earls Court Motor Show in October. The basic outline was complete, but the ex-Ford man added his own touches, including the boot shut-line that swept around the filler cap at the base of the rear screen and along the car's flanks.

Though the design was well received, just two cars were built, rather than the once-envisaged six. Apparently, Sir William Lyons was impressed with Karen's makeover on the Daimler's unhappy visage, but his interest didn't extend to taking up an option on the design, as it would provide too much competition for the Jaguar E-type. However, one interested onlooker was Ray Wiggins, managing director of the Reliant Motor Company.

Ogle

Wiggins was keen to dispel his firm's septuagenarian image and move away from merely producing economy trikes, but Reliant's initial stab at building a sports car had proved a costly embarrassment. Indescribably ugly, the Reliant Sabre had met with howls of derision from motoring hacks when launched in '62, and remained resolutely glued to showroom floors. A deal was struck whereby the Ogle SX250's body would be mated to a Sabre chassis, and after much development, the Reliant Scimitar GT was born two years later.

By this time, Ogle Design had become a styling house, car production having fallen by the wayside. The SX1000 moulds were

In late '66 the rights to the SX1000 passed to John Fletcher who initiated his own restyle.

sold in late-'66 to boat builder Norman Fletcher who, in a rather misguided move, installed large Perspex-cowled headlights and Austin 1800 tail-light clusters. The Fletcher GT, as it was now dubbed, appeared at the '67 Racing Car Show, the display model being a lightweight racer built for works Mini ace, John Handley. But demand was minimal and, with BMC predictably unwilling to supply parts, Fletcher soon lost interest and canned the project after just four cars had been built.

Following the appearance of the Scimitar GT, Ogle swiftly established a fruitful working relationship with Reliant, the subsequent assignment being

The Reliant Scimitar grew from the ashes of the Ogle Daimler project.

the Triplex GTS (Glazing Test Special). Appearing at the '65 Motor Show, this handsome shooting-brake was designed to demonstrate the use of glass in motorcars. Based on a GT, with Triplex heat-absorbing safety glass throughout, the GTS was subsequently bought by HRH Prince Philip who later sold it on, tiring of being so conspicuous. A further variation on the theme appeared in '68, with a larger windscreen and opaque roof panel, plus four concealed headlights.

The Triplex GTS and its younger sibling acted as forerunners for Ogle and Reliant's most acclaimed enterprise – the Scimitar GTE. With GT sales failing to reach expectations, Karen mooted a bold sporting estate car as its replacement. Wiggins gave his full support, and the resultant prototype proved the biggest draw at the '70 Motor Show. The GTE proved a controversial design, and *Autocar*

Tom Karen was hired to run the company in 1962, and remains there nearly four decades on.

ran an entire editorial on the car in which half the staff raved about its bold silhouette, the other half railing against its upswept swage-line and vast rear screen. Even so, the car quickly established itself as a favourite of society scions including Princess Anne, a number of rip-off merchants and copyists cribbing from Karen's handiwork over the course of the next decade.

But if the GTE was a radical concept, it appeared positively tame when compared to the Tamworth firm's other debutant. Reliant had purchased rival three-wheeler producer Bond in '68, inheriting a range of lacklustre and antiquated designs. Keen to inject a little sparkle, Karen suggested a sporting three-wheeler, codenamed Rascal. When it finally appeared, nobody was quite

The remarkable Ogle Sotheby Special featured 22 tail lights and Sundym glass.

The trippy Bond Bug three-wheeler – styled for Reliant by Ogle Design.

prepared for the bright orange wedge, now known as the Bond Bug. It proved an instant hit with hip young blades, and over 2000 of these retina-worrying, tangerine-coloured devices were built up until '74.

However, Ogle wasn't entirely dependent on Reliant. In 1970, John Ogier held talks with tobacco company W.D. & H.O. Wills with a view to building a concept car that would act as a promotional tool for its Sotheby Special brand. Studies were underway early the following year using an Aston Martin DBS platform. The donor car's outer skin was removed, the nose lengthened and tail shortened. The Karen-styled glassfibre body was then draped over the inner skeleton, the dramatic outline featuring extensive brushed aluminium, and no less than 22 rear lights. Finished in dark blue with gold pinstriping, the Sotheby Special's cabin featured Danish moquette, with tubes framing the seats and instrument panel, along with expansive Triplex Sundym heat-filtering glass. Most unusual feature, however, was the single rear seat, sited diagonally to provide ample head and legroom for an adult.

After its show career was over, the car was bedecked in sponsorship decals before being given to motor racing legend Graham Hill, whose nascent Grand Prix team was similarly branded. Though originally intended as a one-off, a second car was subsequently built, after much persuasion, for a wealthy widow who lived near Aston Martin's Newport Pagnell factory.

Ogle Design would go on to pen further Reliants and become renowned for its award-winning truck cab designs, but the Sotheby Special effectively marked the end of its days as an English coachbuilder. Though David Ogle failed to realise his dream, his legacy lives on.

Peerless

The Warwick GT was happiest when viewed from the front. Around 40 or so examples were built.

The Peerless coupé should have been a success. All the ingredients were there – well-proportioned styling, commendable build-quality, and support from Standard-Triumph which supplied componentry. Unfortunately, bickering directors and over-ambition killed the Peerless stone dead.

The story begins in 1956, when successful hotel owner and restaurateur James Brynes dreamed of campaigning a competition car bearing his own name, with a view to selling replicas to fellow enthusiasts should it prove competitive. Brynes, universally known as Jimmy, was determined to realise his vision, and approached experienced specials builder Bernie Rodger to help. Rodger had a proven pedigree, having penned, among others, the famed Beart-Rodger racer. However, somewhere along the line, plans for a new competition machine went west as both men believed that there was more chance of selling a road-going GT.

There was never any doubt over what mechanics the car was going to use. Virtually the entire board of Standard-Triumph dined at Brynes's Warwick restaurant, and the rugged TR3 supplied its engine and running gear for the prototype, based around a multi-tubular semi-spaceframe and clothed in an amorphous alloy skin. Completed in early '57, the new, and as yet unnamed, coupé exceeded all expectations. It was pretty, if a little strangely proportioned from some angles, and could top 120mph, with the 0–60mph dash taking a whisker under ten seconds.

In an effort to get some objective input during the development phase, Brynes loaned the prototype to his former army friend John Gordon. A long-time racing man (he had competed in a 4CLT Maserati among other cars), Gordon was at this time running a thriving Rolls-Royce coachbuilding firm,

Peerless GT	
Made	Slough, Berkshire
Engine	Front-mounted, water-cooled 1991cc ohv 'four'
Construction	Semi-spaceframe chassis with glassfibre body
Top speed	111mph
0–60mph	10.6 seconds
Price new	£1048 (1958)

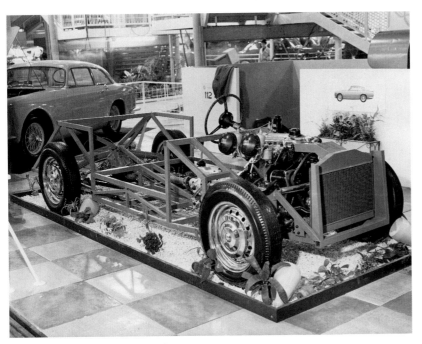

A Peerless chassis displays its robust construction. The glassfibre body was non-structural.

A Peerless splashes its way to 16th place at Le Mans in '58. After the race, the car was driven back to England.

rebodying pre-war machines with wooden-framed shooting-brake bodies. Though impressed by the prototype, he wasn't altogether convinced that it had a future, believing that the car was too small to succeed. Brynes concurred, which led to the construction of an all-new prototype with a wider track and de Dion rear end.

With John Gordon now on-board, this new, larger 2+2 was displayed at the '57 Paris Motor Show, where it was viewed with great interest by Standard-Triumph's top brass, including Harry Webster. With an agreement for the supply of componentry, all that was needed was somewhere to build the cars. A former Jaguar dealership was found in Slough, from where the embryonic Peerless Motors was born. There then remained the small matter of tooling up for production. On the same trading estate was an engineering firm headed by an ardent car enthusiast who agreed to make the chassis and axle tubes. Aluminium bodies would have been too costly and laborious to build, so the move was made to glassfibre, the moulding work also subcontracted out to a local firm, James Whitson Ltd.

Interest in the newcomer at the Paris show suggested that the Peerless would be a keen seller. One American distributor called for 80 cars per month, and the first three off the line in May '58 were warmly received by the press. In order to capitalise on the media attention, two cars entered in the following month's Le Mans 24-hour race (one as reserve). With support from Standard-Triumph, these cars (the fifth and sixth made) were virtually production-spec, with an oversized petrol tank in each sill and a third in the boot, while the suspension was lowered slightly and the compression ratio was raised. Peter Jopp and Percy Crabb covered 259 laps at an average of 84mph to finish sixteenth overall.

This result succeeded in raising the car's profile, and soon Peerless Motors was in need of larger premises to meet demand. A new facility was found in Slough, and Peerless Cars Ltd was formed to handle sales. Production was soon running at five cars a week, despite the high price – £990 plus £500 purchase tax, while a TR3 could have been yours for less. But the car was still too expensive to build.

The number of individual moulds needed to build a single body reached around 57 so, in an effort to simplify the process, the new Phase II model of '59 used a single mould for the bodyshell, with the floor, boot interior and dashboard bonded in before removal from the mould. The new variant was considerably lighter and more attractive too, thanks to the revised frontal treatment which featured recessed headlights and a conventional grille in place of the previous 'P' emblem that adorned the air intake.

Unfortunately, trouble was brewing in the board room. Robert Thornton

100

A Warwick GT displays its rather unnecessary vestigial fins.

had bought a stake in the firm, prompting John Gordon and sales manager Sam Roston to resign, which predictably caused unease amongst component suppliers. The firm quickly fell into receivership, although the remaining directors managed to resume production of a sort under the new Bernard Rodgers Developments banner, from a new factory in Horton, Berkshire. The existing Peerless was reworked with a new bonnet that pivoted forward in one piece for access to the 2-litre Triumph 'four', while the roofline was squared-off in a rather misguided move, with small fins added along the guttering.

The newly renamed Warwick GT was offered for £1666 with leather trim, Webasto sunroof and wire wheels as options. But at that price, it was in elite company, and *The Motor* was especially damning of its lack of refinement. Nonetheless, a steady trickle of cars emerged from the new factory, and a US distribution set-up was formed through Brian Shier in White Plains, New York. Around this time, a young American enthusiast, studying at Cambridge University, installed an alloy small-block Buick V8 in his Warwick, prompting this intriguing Anglo-American crossbreed to be offered for public consumption as the GT350L from '61. Capable of 140mph and 0–60mph in 6.8 seconds, one example was campaigned with success in conjunction with Tunex Conversions, winning the Bardahl Trophy for saloon cars.

But this success wasn't enough to save the marque. In January '61, Bernie Rodger had quit, with a number of senior staff swiftly following suit. Jim Brynes was spending much of his time attending to his other, non-automotive business interests, and the doors closed for good in October '61, followed by a compulsory winding-up order in January '62. Plans to produce the car in Dublin came to naught and, following the liquidation sale, remaining components were turned into cars by D.A. Mallard Ltd of Middlesex. Engineer Chris Lawrence, of Deep Sanderson and Monica fame, also built a Peerless/Warwick crossbreed for his father, amusingly dubbed the Peewick.

Exact production figures are unknown, but it is widely believed that around 250 Phase 1 and 50 Phase 2 Peerless cars were made in total, along with 40 or so Warwicks.

Warwick GT's one-piece flip-up front end reveals Triumph TR power.

Peerless

Piper

More than 30 years on, the shape of the Piper GTT still appears futuristic. A model was wind-tunnel tested during the design phase – something of a rarity for a small-scale car producer.

Piper GTT	
Made	Wokingham, Berkshire
Engine	Front-mounted, water-cooled 1599cc ohv 'four'
Construction	Semi-spaceframe with backbone and glassfibre body
Top speed	110mph
0–60mph	8 seconds
Price new	£1435 (1970)

Perhaps more than any other specialist sports car marque, Piper has suffered a reputation for poor quality and lack of considerate design. Pipers look good, and handle even better, but drive one in hot weather and you're made to feel like an oven-ready chicken, the expansive glass area and woeful lack of ventilation conspiring to flambé the driver. And then there's the car's ride, which loosens the driver's fillings on anything other than the smoothest of roads. But this is to denigrate a marque that went down its own route rather than following the crowd, and would undoubtedly have been more successful but for continuous and crippling financial instability.

The Piper marque was born at Cambell's Garage in Hayes, Kent in 1965, the brainchild of George Henrotte who had previously found success as a racing driver and team manager with the Chequered Flag Gemini Formula Junior team. Together with business partner Bob Gayler, Henrotte formed a tuning firm under the Piper banner. They drifted into building cars more by accident than design, after a customer requested they produce for him a small, mid-engined sports-racing car. Intended purely as a one-off, it proved a modestly successful racer, prompting three more orders. One was constructed for American journalist and Trans-Am legend Jerry Titus, complete with a small-block Buick V8 engine. Another example went to Bobby Bell, of famed sports car dealership Bell & Collville, which proved blindingly quick in British national sports car events.

Around this time, the fledgling concern moved to Dan Gurney's former All American Racing F1 factory in Ashford to concentrate on engine development. Robin Sherwood, who had bought the ex-Gerry Hall car, agreed

Jerry Titus's Piper-Buick sports-racer at Heathrow awaiting transportation to America.

terms to take over the racing car side of the business, but Henrotte stipulated that he should also take on the road car project that was underway. A trio of club racers had approached Piper requesting a new, ultra-lightweight sports car to accept the running gear, engine and transmission from their race-prepared Austin-Healey Sprites. Ultimately, they dropped out as the prototype neared completion, but another customer invested in the project, former Brabham and McLaren man Tony Hilder being charged with the design and development of the car – dubbed the GTT.

The son of artist Roland Hilder, the young engineer designed a backbone chassis that followed Lotus Elan practice in having a Y-shaped front section onto which the engine and transmission were mounted, and a T-structure at the back to take the Sprite-derived rear suspension. The major difference compared to its more established Cheshunt rival was that the chassis was a tubular spaceframe rather than being pressed from sheet steel. Despite lacking any formal styling training, Hilder penned a radical and hugely attractive body for the frame, and a quarter-scale model was wind-tunnel tested at the Kingston College of Technology. This was then something of a rarity in itself, as aerodynamic testing for small-scale car producers usually involved guesswork or attaching tufts of wool to a car and watching which direction they moved at speed. The final shape was wildly futuristic yet free of image-conscious fads. More than 30 years on, the shape still appears futuristic.

A bestriped GTT on display at the 1970 Racing Car Show.

A full-size mock-up was displayed at the January '67 Racing Car Show, where Piper attracted some 700 enquiries, which translated into more than a dozen orders, although half of them requested Ford power. After just six Sprite-based cars had been completed, Sherwood became increasingly sidetracked with an ambitious Group 6 GTR racing car project that promised much yet delivered little. This ultra-sleek machine was of monocoque construction, made of plywood sandwiched in glassfibre to give a strong, yet featherweight structure. The first car was powered by a 2-litre BMW 'four', but proved unreliable. Nevertheless, two cars were entered in the '69 Le Mans 24-hour classic

Piper

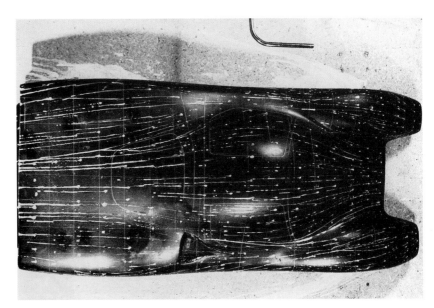

A Group 6 GTR racing car body undergoing aerodynamic testing.

A Piper P2 seen here with the stillborn Formula 3 racer.

with Oldsmobile V8 power, but only one made it to the event, and was withdrawn before the start. Development of the car was beyond the firm's meagre means, and only four examples were produced, one subsequently being converted into a road car. The firm also toyed with manufacturing open-wheel single-seaters, building a highly distinctive Formula 3 car with extensive use of melamine as a weight-saving device. Though on paper the car looked competitive, it never made it trackside, as sports car manufacture took precedence.

Only a handful of GTTs, with 1.6-litre Ford power and a mix of Triumph and Ford running gear, were produced before Sherwood's untimely death in December '69, and the story would have ended there but for the intervention of Piper's works manager Bill Atkinson and fellow employee Tony Waller.

Together, they kept the company afloat, introducing a new variation on the theme, the P2 (for Phase 2), in 1971. From the outside, it was distinguishable from it predecessor by twin headlights in place of the previous oblong affairs, plus new tail-light clusters. The most telling difference, however, was the insertion of six inches into the wheelbase. Underneath, revisions included the adoption of a Ford Capri rear axle and a stiffened chassis. The cabin was left largely untouched, retaining the fixed windows of double-curvature Perspex but with a removable sunroof – a much-needed addition, as effective cockpit heat dissipation had been lacking in earlier models.

Sadly, the company fell into liquidation the same year, a strike at Ford resulting in a lack of engines and subsequent delays in production. Atkinson and Waller revived the marque shortly thereafter under the Embrook Engineering banner, production moving to new Lancashire premises. The P2 underwent a minor facelift, with pop-up headlights making the car look even more space-aged. But Piper's fortunes failed to change for the better, Embrook turning to manufacturing glassfibre bathtubs and jacuzzis to make ends meet. The last P2 was completed in 1974, the once-mooted revival of the GTR racer for road use on a VW Beetle floorpan perhaps mercifully coming to nothing. Less than 100 cars had been built bearing the Scottish piper logo, of which a remarkably high percentage still survive. And the name still lives, in spirit at least, with Piper Cams, the original tuning business remaining unaffected throughout the torturous saga, and latterly finding fame for its twin-cam conversions on Ford pushrod engines.

Although the GTR was intended for Le Mans, it never made the start.

Piper

Probe

The Probe 15 was the lowest car in the world, sitting just 29 inches above the ground, with entry by sliding roof.

In the rarefied world of British specialist sports car designers, one name continues to garner praise from all quarters – Dennis Adams. Famed for penning the Marcos 1800, he has created more than 20 hugely original machines in a 40-year career, ranging from sports-racing cars to luxury off-roaders; micro-cars to '30s-style roadsters. After splitting with Marcos in the early '60s, Dennis, along with his younger brother and long-time cohort Peter, set up a design consultancy. They were responsible for a raft of distinctive and highly unusual projects, which included a single-seater commuter car that could be parked on its tail, and a low-slung sports-car intended for production in Israel. But, by far and away the most notorious of their creations, was the short-lived Probe series.

Unveiled to a shell-shocked audience on the Marcos stand at the '69 Racing Car Show, the Adams Design Probe 15 (so named as it was Dennis's fifteenth car design) was the undoubted star, the motoring press lurching into hyperbole overload over the outlandish newcomer. And it isn't difficult to see why. Intended as an 'investigation into the extremes of styling', it was the lowest car in the world, the top of its domed roof sitting just 29 inches above the ground. The Probe 15 (its name was later abbreviated by the press) was so low that doors were neither necessary nor possible. To gain entry to the avant-garde cockpit you simply slid back the roof over the rear deck and stepped aboard. The roof could then be left back for open motoring. Other unusual features included electric pop-up headlights, adjustable pedals, a steering wheel with a two-inch dish, and a massive near-flat windscreen that visibly shimmied in the centre through being so close to the horizontal. However, beneath the science-fiction facade was nothing more exotic than Hillman Imp running gear mounted

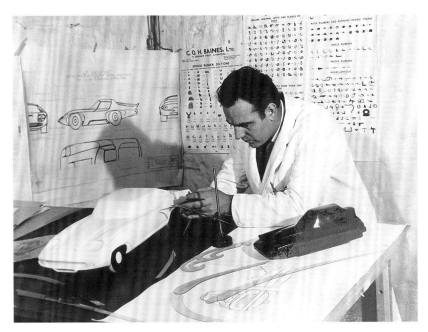

aboard the plywood and glassfibre monocoque. With a top speed of around 80mph (and not the originally quoted 120mph), it lacked the performance to back up its supercar looks, and the mooted production run was dropped as the Adams brothers turned their attentions to creating a more powerful variant – the Probe 16.

A development of the 15, this new model sported a new upper body section with a glass roof that slid back on runners at the press of a button. A lofty 34 inches high, it was marginally more practical (all things being relative), and with its mildly tuned Austin 1800 engine mounted amidships, was considerably faster than its predecessor. Hideously expensive at £3650, the first Probe

Dennis Adams, seen here at work on a Bentley coupé prototype, was responsible for the design of the Probe 15.

16 went to singer Jim Webb, the second to bass player Jack Bruce, who were typical of the clientele the car attracted. Its fame spread further still following an appearance in Stanley Kubrick's seminal movie *A Clockwork Orange*. (A spooky co-incidence, as Dennis Adams later designed a clockwork apple toy for Corgi that sprouted plastic maggots!)

The stillborn Autocars of Israel Austin 1300-based prototype, forerunner of the Probe 15.

With proposed funding from an enthusiastic businessman, work then commenced on what would be the definitive production Probe – the 2001. Though originally intended for V8 power, this latest variant ultimately retained the hefty BMC 1800 motor, enlarged to 2 litres. The 16's body was further revised, with a steeper windscreen helping to raise the overall height to a

Probe

The launch of the Probe 15 saw journalists launch into hyperbole overload. It is not difficult to see why.

Beneath the science-fiction facade of the Probe 15 was nothing more exotic than Hillman Imp running gear.

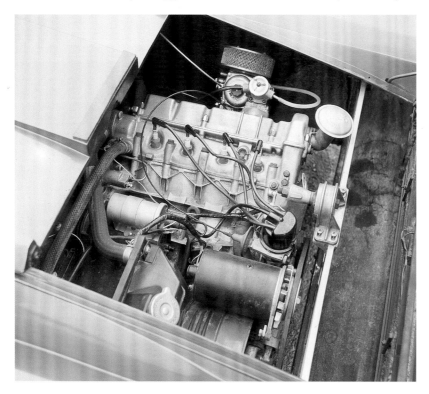

heady 37 inches. The rear styling in particular aped that of an earlier sports-racer which Dennis Adams had styled for the Anglia Racing Organisation in conjunction with John Tojeiro. Electrical gimmickry went a stage further, with not only a powered sliding roof (in place of the once-envisaged gullwing doors), but electric seats that slid back and upwards, allowing occupants to step onto the floor on entry, rather than the seats themselves as with the 16. Just above the seats sat an external aerofoil encasing a sturdy roll-over bar. The first car was completed in April 1970.

But the mystery benefactor swiftly disappeared, leaving the Adams brothers to go it alone while simultaneously designing yet another Probe, this time a wedge-shaped five-seater sporting estate, dubbed the 7000 in deference to its 7-litre Oldsmobile V8 engine. Unlike its smaller siblings, this new model sported conventional doors on its timber monocoque, with Jaguar E-type front and rear suspension, and a central driving position. Sponsored by The *Daily Telegraph Magazine* design scheme, a mock-up was displayed at the 1970 London Motor Show. Sadly, without the necessary funding to continue developing both cars, the firm soon slipped into liquidation.

The production tally was pitiful, with just a lone Probe 15, three 16s and three to five 2001s, giving a grand total of just eight to ten genuine Probes. The 7000 was

PROBE 2001

STYLING & DESIGN BY ADAMS DESIGNS
MANUFACTURE BY PROBE MOTOR CO. LTD.

The Probe 2001 would prove to be the definitive production Probe, although only a handful were built.

apparently scrapped almost as soon as the mock-up was completed. The Adams brothers turned to crafting bespoke wrought ironwork, but that wasn't the end of the story. A Dutch Volkswagen dealer had approached the Adams brothers in 1970 with a view to selling Probes with Beetle running gear in Holland. A 15 body was widened and lengthened by six inches for the new application, but the project was swiftly abandoned, the unfinished prototype passing to Jonathon Wilde. The Wiltshire enthusiast completed the car, modifying the roof with Perspex gullwing doors, and incorporating faired-in headlights, along with a prominent bonnet bulge to house two spare wheels, which did nothing for the car's looks. Powered by an asthmatic 1.2-litre flat-four, the Wilde-Probe proved painfully slow and was ultimately scrapped.

Meanwhile, Ayrshire firm W.T. Nugent Engineering bought the rights to the 2001, and commissioned Peter Adams to produce a further dozen monocoques, although it appears that none were ever built into cars. Another enterprising enthusiast, Peter Timpson, bought the moulds to the widened Probe 15 and launched the much-modified Centaur in 1974, which ironically outsold all the Probes, around 25 being made up until 1977. Timpson also produced a one-off spaceframed version of the 2001, dubbed the Timeire, and a drastically altered 16, dubbed the Pulsar.

With the benefit of hindsight, it seems almost inevitable that the Probe series was doomed from the outset, as they were perhaps too adventurous for British tastes. Even so, the designs still look outlandish, which is a testament to the Adams brothers' artistic talents.

Probe 15	
Made	Bradford-on-Avon, Wiltshire
Engine	Rear-mounted, air-cooled, all-alloy 875cc 'four'
Construction	Timber monocoque with glassfibre outer skin
Top speed	80mph
0–60mph	14 seconds
Price new	£950 (1969)

Probe

Rochdale

The featherweight Rochdale Olympic's streamlined body hid Riley 1.5 running gear. *(Malcolm McKay)*

Rochdale Olympic Phase II	
Made	Rochdale, Yorkshire
Engine	Front-mounted, water-cooled 1499cc ohv 'four'
Construction	Glassfibre monocoque
Top speed	115mph
0–60mph	10.2 seconds
Price new	£735 (1964)

Rochdale continues to suffer as the poor relation of the likes of Lotus, Ginetta and Elva, yet it was one of the most consistently adventurous marques of the '50s and early '60s. Rochdale Motor Panels & Engineering was formed immediately after the Second World War by two friends, Harry Smith and Frank Butterworth, who began as panel beaters. Yet the firm was to transcend the specials boom into the realms of technologically advanced GT cars, and would undoubtedly have scaled giddier heights had not fate intervened.

Keen motor sport enthusiasts, it wasn't long before Smith and Butterworth became involved in the burgeoning 750 Motor Club scene, producing a neat cigar-shaped aluminium body to clothe Austin Seven chassis from '48. These beautifully crafted bodies were originally ash-framed, but the duo soon switched to aluminium monocoques that cost a hefty £300. Even so, around 50 found homes over the ensuing four years.

Forming alloy bodies with complex curves proved time consuming and laborious, so the partners took to learning about glassfibre, producing their first bodyshell from this material in March 1954. Priced at £75, the bulbous MkVI was an instant hit with the competition fraternity and could be adapted to fit any number of chassis, from Ford Popular and Morris Eight to pre-war Triumph Vitesse and even Paramount, around 150 being sold up until '61.

By 1955, two rather more attractive bodies had been added to the line up. The C-type allegedly owed its bold lines to John Coombs's Connaught ALSR that had received remedial work at Rochdale, moulds having been taken off it during an overnight stay. Ironically, one such 'shell graced Peter Bell's 1.5-

110

litre Connaught that was often campaigned by Formula 3 ace Les Leston. With its steeply scalloped front wings and aggressively haunched hind-quarters, styling was reminiscent of the Aston Martin DB3S sports-racer, and it soon proved popular with competition-minded specials builders. As did the F-type offered for £55, another one-piece shell that required the builder to cut his own cockpit, wing edges, bonnet and boot lid. The prototype body was sold to Cedric Brierly for his Victoria-Climax, another gracing Alex MacMillan's Bristol-Barb.

Never happy to rest on their laurels, Smith and Butterworth then conceived the ST (Sports Tourer) in 1956, which was sold with inner wheelarches, front bulkhead and floor sections bonded in so it would slip on to any post-'37 Ford 8 chassis. Rochdale's adverts boasted of how the ST body could 'easily be fitted by any handyman' to its new application, claiming that a car could

Rochdale's Type F was a favourite with the competition fraternity.

The curvaceous Rochdale GT predated the Olympic by three years.

Rochdale

The pretty Riviera was essentially a GT with the roof removed and a wider, flatter grille. *(Malcolm McKay)*

be built with little more than a tool set and an electric drill, which was perhaps a little optimistic. While the bonnet and doors were supplied ready-fitted, a fair amount of massaging was still required to get everything to fit. And then there was the leisurely performance. The adoption of a new body was not about to transform a decrepit Ford into a road burner, while the deplorable beam axle suspension was anything but sporting.

While the ST sold steadily, it never proved as popular as the partners had once envisaged, being overshadowed by the two subsequent models. Realising the latent demand for a more practical kit for the family man, Rochdale introduced the GT in 1957, and immediately struggled to cope with demand. Styled by student Richard Parker, this curvaceous coupé aped the lines of the F-type, but was an infinitely more cohesive design, the body being rigid enough to be fitted to an unboxed chassis. It came complete with a curved windscreen and the tops of Morris Minor doors to give opening windows and quarterlights, features previously unheard of in the specials arena. As were moulded-in wheel arches, battery box, bulkhead, and dashboard complete with glovebox. Priced at £140 with doors, windows and bonnet already fitted, around 1350 were sold, most fitted to proprietary Ford chassis (the firm offered a strengthened frame for £27), although a handful were applied to more sophisticated Buckler, Alexis and even Cooper frames.

Such was the GT's success, that Rochdale's works swiftly became a hive of activity. In late-'59, *Autosport* reported that: 'The factory now has 21 employees with an assembly line of six bodies on the floor at any one time. Delivery dates for these 'shells is 14 weeks at the moment but it is hoped to halve this in the very near future by increasing the production line and producing another mould.' Even so, the partners sought out other untapped

112

The Olympic Phase II appeared after the disastrous factory fire that almost wiped out the marque.

areas of the market, unveiling its pretty Riviera in September 1959. Essentially a GT with the roof removed and a wider, flatter grille, this new variant was a more upmarket kit, based, as ever, on Ford running gear. But, for all its virtues and its comprehensive specification, it failed to strike a chord with the punters and achieved only a fraction of the GT's success.

From 1960, Rochdale offered its own chassis with split-beam independent front suspension, and a Watt's linkage at the rear, making for a relatively supple ride and improved handling over the boxed Ford efforts. But, such was the glut of purpose-made chassis on offer from firms such as Buckler, L.M. Bellamy and Bowden Engineering, Rochdale's effort found few takers, possibly fewer than 25.

Convinced that the specials boom was likely to crash, Smith and Butterworth decided that Rochdale's future lay in producing an all-new model, with modern running gear and superior dynamics to the floppy old Ford-based kits. They launched the brave new Olympic on an unsuspecting world in 1960 (when the Games were being held in Rome). Styled by Richard Parker, Rochdale's new baby broke with tradition in being a glassfibre monocoque, only Lotus's complex and financially draining Elite being similarly constructed. And the Lotus affair used a significant amount of metal reinforcement, while the only steel used in the Olympic's shell was a roll-bar incorporated into the windscreen pillars. *Motoring News* dedicated their cover to the newcomer asking: 'Is this a new Alfa?' Presumably the writer didn't have his lenses in as the car's silhouette was decidedly Porsche-esque, rather than Italianate. The Olympic's streamlined body hid Riley 1.5 running gear, endowing the featherweight coupé with a top speed of 105mph, the 0–60mph dash taking a whisker under 12 seconds. Front suspension was robbed from the Morris Minor or Riley, a torsion bar system with rack-and-pinion steering, and all mountings carried on a steel tubular subframe that was bonded to the inner wings and floorpan. At the back, radius arms and telescopic dampers located the rear axle.

The Olympic Phase II's cabin was among the plushest of any specialist sports car of the era.

Road testers eulogised over the newcomer, *The Motor* stating: 'Driving the prototype emphasised the rigidity of the construction, none of the body shake found in glassfibre 'shells being evident. There was very little wind noise and the top speed was commendably high.' But disaster was waiting around the corner, as a fire ripped through the factory in February '61, destroying all the moulds and jigs within. This terrible setback caused Rochdale to abandon all the early models and concentrate exclusively on reviving Olympic production.

Using 'shells that had escaped the fire, new moulds were created at new premises at Littledale Mill. Months passed before manufacture recommenced, by which time many orders were cancelled. However, Rochdale bounced back, introducing the Phase II Olympic at the '63 London Racing Car Show, with Ford 116 Classic (later Cortina GT) power, and Triumph Spitfire-derived front suspension complete with nine-inch disc brakes. Top speed was now a highly commendable 115mph, with 0–60mph taking 11.2 seconds, this hike in performance aided by a reduction in glassfibre thickness which saved 150lbs. Outwardly identifiable by its bigger bonnet and opening rear hatchback, the Phase II was better made than its predecessor, particular attention having been given to addressing criticisms of the cabin furniture and layout. Though it proved popular, the impetus had gone. Smith and Butterworth, weary of dealing with component suppliers and appeasing customers who could not get part A to mate with part B, began to wind down production. Car manufacture swiftly became little more than an occasional sideline as the partners moved into the more profitable area of moulding heater ducting. Rochdale advertisements gradually disappeared from the motoring monthlies, and the Phase II was never actively promoted from the mid-'60s.

Reflecting on the Olympic, Harry Smith latterly believed that too little attention was initially paid to the quality of the interior trim, misjudging the type of customer they were attracting. This, he felt, undoubtedly blunted sales. In total, around 250 Phase I Olympics, along with 150 Phase II cars, were built up until '67, although the model was still technically available until the early '70s. Just ten were sold in '67, the same number the following year, and very few thereafter. The last monocoque was produced in 1973 after much persuasion. The moulds and jigs passed to a consortium of Olympic owners in the late-'70s who still preserve them. That the survival rate for this distinctive sporting coupé is so high (around 170 still exist) is a testimony to the integrity of a vastly underrated design.

Tornado

Tornado's Typhoon wasn't the prettiest of '50s kit cars, but it was one of the best made. Its thoughtful design was a revelation.

THE TORNADO SPORTSBRAKE

Sports car performance, handling and safety with shooting brake capacity.

CARS
TORNADO **LIMITED**
RICKMANSWORTH HERTFORDSHIRE
Telephones: Rickmansworth 5176 or 5006

If ever there was a problem facing specials manufacturers in the '50s, it was telling the world about their products. Tornado was the exception, employing a press agent to boost its profile, and using motor sport to keep the marque firmly in the limelight. In six years of production from 1958 to 1964, Tornado produced over 500 cars, and with proper funding that figure could have been multiplied several times over.

Together with friend Anthony Bullen, Bill Woodhouse conceived a Ford Popular-based kit car – the Tornado Typhoon – that was different from most of its rivals in having a custom-made frame, as opposed to retaining the donor car's chassis. Bullen designed a tubular affair consisting of two, widely spaced 3-inch-diameter tubes in 16-gauge drawn steel, with smaller crossmembers and risers to accept Armstrong telescopic dampers all round. The donor car's front axle was split to make swing-axle independent suspension, the engine mounted seven inches further back relative to the original Ford. Woodhouse concentrated on the styling, producing an oddly proportioned but beautifully made 2+2 that was sold with underpan mouldings, and incorporated front and rear bulkheads, seat pans and transmission tunnel. Inner wheel arches were provided, doors were double-skinned, and the one-piece bonnet flipped up for engine access. In a time when the average kit car was supplied as a bare shell requiring a great deal of cutting and re-engineering, the Typhoon's thoughtful design was a revelation.

With production underway in mid-'58, the fledgling Tornado Cars received a major setback when its backers attempted a boardroom coup, believing (correctly) that industrial mouldings would be more profitable. Woodhouse's parents provided a timely injection of funds for the firm to continue. By 1959,

115

the first two-seater Typhoon was built, which was considerably neater than its longer sister. A lightweight competition version was also added to the line-up and, by April of that year, around 60 kits had been sold, including one to Thailand.

In late-'59, Woodhouse set to work on a new, more substantial ladderframe design, with the Standard Ten supplying wishbone front suspension and a live rear axle located by a Panhard Rod, two lower trailing arms and an offset upper arm. This new chassis came into play on the new Tempest, a four-seater GT which, when tested by Tony Bostock in *Car Mechanics*, September 1960,

A Tornado Tempest with Touring bonnet. This four-seater GT was launched in 1960.

received a rave review. He stated: 'The car frequently reached an estimated speed of 85mph and handled remarkably well on very wet corners.' Power came from the recently introduced 997cc Ford 105E 'four', with the option of BMC A-series, 948cc Triumph Herald or Ford 109E motors.

While the Tempest was under development, Woodhouse and Bullen (who was shortly to leave to run a garage in the west country) also produced a larger-engined sports car, using a Tempest chassis adapted to suit a Triumph TR3 engine along with a Ford Zephyr rear axle and Alford & Alder double-wishbone front suspension. The appropriately named Thunderbolt was reportedly capable of 130mph, and was announced for public consumption a month after the Tempest. But new developments did not end there. Later that year, Tornado broke new ground with its Sportsbrake, an estate car variant of the Typhoon that set a trend in car design which was popularised at the end of the decade by Reliant's Scimitar.

The Tornado Sportsbrake predated the Reliant Scimitar sporting estate concept by 12 years.

Amid this flurry of new launches, Tornado entered a team in the 750 Motor Club's Six Hour Relay, with Eric Martin aboard a Thunderbolt, Woodhouse in a Tempest, and Tony Bunce driving a supercharged sidevalve Typhoon. In spite of the handicapping rules, the equipe scooped the winner's trophy. With sales booming, the number of staff at the Rickmansworth factory had grown to 20, with racing enthusiast Colin Hextall joining the firm as a director.

For 1961, Tornado offered a Tempest with independent rear suspension, using a magnesium differential casing, finned aluminium drums for inboard brakes, and meaty uprights, aping the set-up of the Condor Formula Junior single-seaters. By this time, more than 300

Tornado

116

Talisman

The final evolution of the Talisman was one of the most refined specialist sports cars of the day.

Tornado kits had found homes, but the sudden rash of affordable production cars meant that sales were beginning to ebb. Racing was an expensive pastime, and declining sales meant prices had to rise. A kit-form Thunderbolt was virtually the same price as a Ford Consul, and a factory-built example cost near Jaguar XK150 money, while a Tempest could have been yours for the price of a new Austin-Healey 3000. Woodhouse and Hextall attempted to stop the rot by introducing a new, more conventional front end for the Typhoon, which did wonders for its looks but failed to have much of an impact on orders.

To make matters worse, a fire ripped through the laminating shop in late summer '61, moulds for the four-seater Tempest and Thunderbolt being among the casualties. Rather than go to the trouble of retooling, Woodhouse decided to press on with an all-new car – the Talisman – that he had started working on earlier in the year. Its chassis closely resembled that of the competition Tempest but, in order to keep prices down, the rear suspension now incorporated the Triumph Herald differential casing and outboard brakes, though the Tornado's twin trailing arms and lower links with coil spring dampers remained. Following advice from Colin Chapman, coachbuilders Williams & Pritchard were commissioned to interpret Woodhouse's sketches into a full-size body, clothing the prototype chassis.

The finished article (in aluminium, although production cars were bodied in glassfibre) was delivered six weeks before thc '62 Racing Car Show, where it received a warm reception. The handsome, Italianate styling impressed all, as did the specification. Tornado's new baby was the first production car to use a Cosworth-tuned engine as standard, the 1340cc Ford Classic unit sporting a high lift camshaft, gas-flowed cylinder head, two twin-choke Weber carburettors, and a four-branch exhaust manifold. Inside, it was equally well equipped, leather-trimmed Microsell bucket seats, no less than three ashtrays, a lockable glove compartment, and a speedometer that read to a rather optimistic 140mph.

Autocar tested the prototype in July '62, and complained of too much oversteer and intrusive engine noise at speed. However, it couldn't fault the car's performance, recording 0–60mph in 10.2 seconds, and a top speed of

A new development in Sports Car design. Available as a two-seater or "occasional four". The Typhoon is sold in chassis and body form to accept standard Ford 8/10 parts (from 1937 on). No expensive tools . . . no extensive engineering knowledge needed. Simply bolt standard Ford parts to the chassis, and bolt on the stylish fibreglass body and you can have your own Sports Car for as little as £250.

Chassis: Including modifying to independent front suspension.
PRICE £70

Body : Of tough laminated fibreglass construction combining maximum strength and lightness.
PRICE £150

Designed and Built by :—

CARS
TORNADO T **LIMITED**
RICKMANSWORTH HERTFORDSHIRE

Telephone : Rickmansworth 5176 or 5006

Tornado

117

The Talisman should have seen Tornado graduate to being a fully fledged motor manufacturer, but despite the car's high spec, its high price caused its downfall.

102mph. Martyn Watkins from *Autosport* borrowed Talisman number two for a week's trip to the Nürburgring, and was highly enthusiastic, stating: 'The driving position is one of the best I have ever come across.' Covering hundreds of miles at an average of 95mph, he recorded an amazing 30mpg.

This was a brave new world for Tornado, and the emphasis was placed firmly on supplying complete cars, although, at £1299, it faced tough competition from the Triumph TR4, and a less salubrious model – the Talisman Touring – was soon offered in component form. For the '63 Racing Car Show, Tornado introduced a revised model with the latest 1489cc Ford Cortina unit which, when equipped with twin 40DCOE Webers, produced 86bhp at 5500rpm. Chassis tubing was increased in diameter, while the steering rack that had previously transmitted too much vibration was now rubber mounted. Additional sound deadening and silencing was added, making the Talisman one of the most refined specialist sports cars of the day.

Sadly, the high price meant that the Talisman was ultimately doomed to failure. Without much-needed funding, Woodhouse and Hextall attempted to sell the firm as a going concern. Fairthorpe, Standard-Triumph and Reliant considered taking it on, as did Lotus, but Colin Chapman couldn't raise the capital. In the end, millionaire Lister Jaguar racer John Bekaert expressed an interest. His consortium asked Woodhouse to place the company into voluntary liquidation so that he could buy it from the liquidators, a strange policy that angered Tornado's suppliers.

A new company, Tornado Cars (1963) Ltd, was set up under Bekaert. Hextall left to work for Graham Hill, Woodhouse staying on for six months to honour his contract before leaving to head Aston Martin's service department. Talisman prices were raised still further to the point that it was more expensive than the Lotus Elan, and production swiftly came to a standstill. Instead of reacting to the downturn, the consortium moved into selling Volvos, and performance tuning. The Talisman disappeared for good in 1964.

But that wasn't the absolute end of the Tornado. Bekaert experimented with a one-off machine using a Talisman body mated to a Daimler SP250 chassis, in the belief that it might appeal to the American market. It didn't. The final ignominy arrived in October '64 with the announcement of the Tornado-Fiat GT, which was essentially a Fiat 600 with a Ford Cortina 1500GT motor shoehorned up its bulbous rump. This ungodly device could apparently sprint to 60mph in 8.8 seconds, though low gearing restricted it to 98mph overall. Amazingly, four were sold, and Bekaert sprinted his own heavily modified example with some success. Powered by a dry-sumped Martin-tuned 1850cc Ford motor, he scorched to 130mph over the flying kilometre at the '67 Brighton Speed Trials, beating everything bar a Ferrari 250GTO. A bizarre dénouement to a once-prosperous marque.

Tornado Talisman	
Made	Rickmansworth, Hertfordshire
Engine	Front-mounted, water-cooled 1498cc ohv 'four'
Construction	Perimeter frame with glassfibre body
Top speed	109mph
0–60mph	10 seconds
Price new	£1300 (1963)

Trident

The Trident Clipper evolved from the Trevor Fiore-penned TVR Trident. A heavily modified example is shown here.

The Trident marque is inextricably linked with TVR and its descendent Grantura Engineering. By the early '60s, TVR was producing small, lightweight and highly effective little sporting chariots, which were fun to drive and highly capable in competition. The only flaw in the plan was that they were somewhat ugly, with odd proportions and unsightly protrusions. At this time, the Blackpool firm was undergoing a financial reorganisation, and one of the directors, Bernard Williams, was keen to push for a new, more attractively styled model that would appeal to the burgeoning American market. A chance meeting with aspiring designer Trevor Fiore at the London Motor Show set TVR on an adventure that pauperised the firm.

Fiore produced renderings for a new model in open and closed configurations, which bore more than a passing resemblance to a stillborn Lea-Francis project that he had been involved with in 1961. TVR's directors approved of his designs, and Fiore arranged for Italian carrozzeria Fissore to interpret his ideas into a series of prototypes. The first was completed in time for the '65 Geneva Salon where it proved one of the show's stars, *The Daily Telegraph* headlining it as merely 'The most beautiful car in the world.' The basis was a lengthened Griffith chassis with 289cu in Ford small-block V8 power.

Chassis number one was then air-freighted to sometime American distributor Jack Griffith to display at the '65 New York Auto Show. The racing entrepreneur took an instant dislike to the rakish coupé after banging his head against the inner roof on the drive back from John F. Kennedy Airport, and wanted nothing more to do with the car: a major blow to TVR. Nonetheless, the company pressed on with development, commissioning Fissore to build a further three prototypes, including a lone convertible.

The Trident's beautifully realised styling grew from the stillborn Trevor Fiore-styled Lea-Francis Francesca.

The definitive Trident Clipper featured Ford V8 power and an Austin-Healey chassis.

However, the TVR Trident never reached production. A dock strike in the US saw several Griffiths stranded on the waterfront. Crippled by the development costs of the Trident, and without any fresh income, Grantura Engineering lurched into bankruptcy. Fiore claimed that he was never paid for his efforts, Fissore only receiving partial recompense. While TVR's future hung in the balance, one of its dealers, Bill Last, struck a deal with the Turinese coachbuilders and took over the project, much to the chagrin of Martin and Arthur Lilley who subsequently rescued the company, claiming that the Trident was their main reason for buying the ailing concern. In the mists of time, acrimony between all parties has clouded the truth concerning who in fact had rights to the project, and the Lilleys and Last continue to declare themselves legal owners of the project.

Last travelled to Turin in late-'65, having arranged a supply of Austin-Healey 3000 chassis from Sankey, the company that supplied BMC, as a replacement for the TVR item. With advice from rally ace Don Morley, who had campaigned Big Healeys with great success, the track was widened, suspension uprated and frame altered to house a 4.7-litre 'Ford Industrial' V8 (or a larger displacement 4950cc version for the Stateside market), which was mounted some six inches further back than the original 3-litre straight-six, to aid weight distribution. Fiore was engaged to rework his original design to accommodate the longer

Trident Clipper II	
Made	Woodbridge, Suffolk
Engine	Front-mounted, water-cooled 5727cc ohv V8
Construction	Cruciform chassis with glassfibre body
Top speed	150mph (manufacturer's claim)
0–60mph	5 seconds (manufacturer's claim)
Price new	£4521 (1971)

When *Motor* evaluated a Venturer, its report was damning, criticising the car's poor handling.

The Trident Venturer wasn't the most obvious competition car, but this example competed in the 1970 World Cup Rally although it did not finish.

wheelbase of the Healey chassis, Fissore charged with making a fresh body buck required to produce the revised shell. But Last and Fissore swiftly fell out over the latter's perceived poor workmanship, and the now independent Grantura Plastics was roped in to produce the new buck – a move that caused more than a little consternation for the Lilleys, TVR's factory being next door!

Following a triumphant debut at the January '67 Racing Car Show, production commenced at Trident Cars's small facility in Market Harborough, with Grantura Plastics producing the bodyshells, although sales activities were based in Woodbridge, Suffolk. In a rationalising move, production and sales were moved under one roof in Suffolk the following year. Visually, the new Trident Clipper differed from the TVR original in several respects, particularly in the styling of the inset headlights fitted in place of the previous pop-up affairs, while the roofline was discernibly steeper.

In 1969, the Austin-Healey was discontinued, forcing Last to scout around for a replacement chassis. After much deliberation he chose the rugged Triumph TR6 perimeter frame, stretched and modified for its new application. A further model was added to the line up, the Venturer being physically identical to its Clipper sister, but with Ford V6 power. From 1972, the car's nose was altered to house rectangular headlights which gave it a unique identity. Trident also produced a small batch of Venturers with TR6 engines, dubbed Tycoons, but this model was swiftly dropped after as few as seven cars had been built. Tridents were always hideously expensive, and in 1971 a Venturer cost more than a Jaguar E-type, the Clipper only marginally cheaper than an Aston Martin DBS – which goes some way to explaining why output never exceeded 25 cars in its best year. That and the lack of coverage the cars received in the motoring magazines.

Bill Last was always reticent with the press, preferring to keep them at arm's length. In period, he never released a Clipper for a road test, and the only contemporary driving impressions of a Trident appeared in a December 1970 issue of *Motor*, which pitched a Venturer against a Triumph TR6, Lotus Europa, Marcos, Lotus Elan SE and TVR Tuscan V6. The verdict was damning, the report stating that: 'On a smooth surface, its outright cornering power

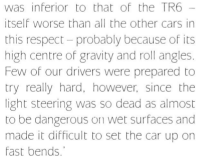

was inferior to that of the TR6 – itself worse than all the other cars in this respect – probably because of its high centre of gravity and roll angles. Few of our drivers were prepared to try really hard, however, since the light steering was so dead as almost to be dangerous on wet surfaces and made it difficult to set the car up on fast bends.'

Considering this criticism, it is all the more remarkable that Trident entertained the notion of competing in the improbable arena of long-distance rallying. A heavily modified Venturer took part in the 1970 London to Mexico World Cup Rally, fielded by two army captains, Christopher Marriott and John Dill.

A late-series Clipper complete with uglified front end and 5.4 litre Ford V8 power.

This ultimately proved to be a disastrous foray, as the car was blighted with suspension problems and missed the ferry to Lisbon, the team being forced to withdraw.

By 1971, Last had formed a small dealer network, the only problem being supplying them with cars. Parts reserves were at best erratic, causing the 30-strong workforce to often substitute components in the build process for anything that was available. That same year, the Clipper's Ford V8 was replaced with a 5.4-litre unit to create the Super 300, but it wasn't enough to save the firm from the financial morass, and Trident Cars went into liquidation in '72. An associate company, Viking Performance, was able to maintain a service agency, the marque entering its wilderness period. Four years passed before Last was in a position to recommence production, with the aid of an injection of funds from an American investor. A new company was formed, the Trident Motor Company, and a new 6-litre variant of the Clipper was displayed at the '76 Earls Court Motor Show. But the marque's time had passed, the firm sinking for good the following year. Around 130 Tridents of all types had been built.

But that wasn't altogether the end of the Fiore-penned silhouette. In the late-'80s, a South African firm, Carousel Engineering, launched a kit-form coupé, based on Ford Cortina running gear, that was pure Trident save for a lightly restyled nose and appalling side skirts. This risible effort was laughably marketed as an Aston Martin DB6 replica!

One final twist was the untrumpeted arrival of an all-new Trident at the '98 Earls Court Motor Show. A beautiful roadster with quad-cam Ford V8 power, this machine had little in common with earlier fare, the only link being that the project instigator once owned a Venturer and liked the name. Little more was heard of this project until the 2000 Motor Show when the car reappeared as the Iceni, powered by a 3-litre straight-six, and engineered by Lola founder Eric Broadley.

Turner

The Turner MkII was launched in 1960 and featured markedly improved trim levels in addition to a redesigned bonnet.

Wolverhampton has never exactly been the epicentre of the automotive universe but, during the early to mid-'50s, numerous small enterprises sprang up to serve the burgeoning production racing car market. Among them was Jack Turner's one-man operation. Having campaigned a highly modified MG K3 with a modicum of success, he built his first bespoke special in 1951, prompting several enthusiasts to commission others. The Sports was built along similar lines to contemporary Tojeiro and Coopers, with a lozenge-shaped twin-tube ladderframe, and all-round independent suspension by transverse leaf springs and lower wishbones. Lightweight wheels made by Turner were optional, and proved popular with the general racing fraternity, John Tojeiro using them on his sports-racers.

Like so many of his contemporaries, Turner supplied only the frame and suspension: it was up to the customer to source components and arrange their own bodywork. Seven Sports chassis were supplied for road use, one of them clothed in achingly pretty Ferrari 166MM-esque coachwork, while an eighth was converted into a Formula 2 racing car for John Webb for the '53 season. Fitted with a 1750cc Lea-Francis engine enlarged to 1960cc, with a twin-plug alloy cylinder head designed by Turner, it also featured an aeronautical SU fuel-injection system adapted for competition use. In this form, the engine apparently pushed out 145bhp at 6500rpm, and drove via an Armstrong-Siddeley pre-selector gearbox to an EMV differential mounted on the chassis.

Webb competed in a number of minor Formula 2 events, proving a mobile chicane to the boys at the sharp end. For '54, a 2.5-litre Alta engine was substituted, but this brought no great change of fortunes, even with

Turner Mk1	
Made	Wolverhampton, West Midlands
Engine	Front-mounted, cast-iron 948cc 'four'
Construction	Perimeter frame with glassfibre body
Top speed	80mph
0–60mph	21.3 seconds
Price new	£782 (1960)

With its Austin A30 running gear and lightweight construction, the Turner 803 predated the Austin-Healey Sprite concept.

professional drivers in the hot seat. The best result was thirteenth from 15 finishers in that year's International Trophy, with Jack Fairman driving: one of the rare occasions that the car actually lasted the distance.

Undeterred by the general lack of results, Turner pressed on with a four-cylinder, water-cooled, double-overhead-cam 500cc engine for Formula 3 applications. Local firm Kieft planned to use these units in the back of its works cars, but was disappointed to discover that the engine only produced 36bhp and so looked elsewhere. All the more ironic then that Turner should change tack and turn his hand to building pure road cars, which would conversely prove so competitive trackside.

In 1955, Turner unveiled the A30 Sports, a two-seater with a slightly gawky, all-enveloping fibreglass body mounted on a light tubular frame. Austin's A30 provided its front suspension, hydro-mech brakes, 803cc four-pot and gearbox, and a live axle suspended by trailing arms and torsion bars. Capable of 81mph, and economical too (45mpg at a constant 50mph), the A30 Sports effectively predated the Austin-Healey Sprite. BMC obviously thought so, as it resolutely refused to supply Turner directly, so he had to buy components from Austin dealers, which only added to the end price, and subsequently blunted sales. Even so, among early customers was former ERA ace Bob Gerrard who drove his example to many class wins in national events, and singer Petula Clark who had hers finished in a none-too-subtle shade of 'Nipple Pink'!

Singer Petula Clark had her Turner 803 painted 'Nipple Pink'.

In 1957, the 803cc-engines car morphed into the 950 Sports, now endowed with fully hydraulic brakes and a 948cc Austin A35 engine. Outwardly it was identical to its predecessor, save for a pair of unnecessary vestigial tailfins that only served to detract from the simplistic silhouette. A few cars were fitted with the 75bhp, 1100cc Coventry Climax FWA engine, and usually came equipped with wire wheels and front disc brakes. Almost all were exported, primarily to America and South Africa.

By late-'59, Turner had made 260 cars, at which point he introduced a new body on the existing chassis. The Sports Mk1's styling was derived from the original 803, but with new,

The Turner 950 Sports, an evolution of the 803, identifiable by its small tail fins.

Pat Ferguson campaigning the famous 'Tatty Turner'. This giant-killer was also raced by Warwick Banks.

more cohesive front and rear ends. The revised body was infinitely more attractive than the original, and there was even a modicum of brightwork – front bumper from an A35, mesh grille cut down from an A55 pick-up, and Standard 10 door handles. Underneath, the Sports Mk1 was virtually identical to its forerunners, with the body mounted to the chassis by 12 securing bolts. The interior was typically stark, with unlined doors, and seats with glassfibre backs bolted directly to the floor; and if you wanted a rev counter or a dash'-mounted grab handle you had to pay a lot more on top of the already steep £815 list price (when a Sprite could have been yours for £613). Front disc brakes were offered as an option on all models, and the 90bhp, 1220cc Coventry Climax FWE engine was available for the Turner-Climax variant.

It was the latter model that truly established Turner's racing credentials. Marque agent Gordon Unsworth of Derby fielded a three-car equipe under the Team Turner banner between 1960 and '63. One of these machines was unpainted for its first outing, and picked up the unfortunate soubriquet of 'Tatty Turner'. It was to become one of the most successful club racers of the period, when driven by Pat Ferguson and future BMC works driver Warwick Banks.

Criticisms of the Mk1's stark nature were partially addressed with the MKII launched in 1960, which featured markedly improved trim levels, along with a restyled bonnet. There was even the option of a glassfibre hard top. The original A30/A35 front suspension was replaced by a Triumph Herald coil spring and double wishbone layout. The main change was the gradual switch from BMC to Ford engines, including the 1340cc 109E unit, while Climax FWA/E engines remained available.

Turner's southern agent, Alexander Engineering of Haddenham, Buckinghamshire, offered its own performance-enhancing tweaks, its speciality being a BMC A-series with a crossflowed cylinder head. The firm had enjoyed considerable success in saloon car racing with its modded Austin A40, and this expertise was used to great effect on Turners – one of the firm's demonstrators topped 105mph with nonchalant ease.

Turner

The New GT TURNER

Quality - Performance - Distinction

The pretty Turner GT was styled by marque founder Jack Turner, but just nine were made.

With confidence fortified by audacity, Alexander then attempted to produce its own Turner-based car. Styled by Tim Fry (also responsible for the Elva Courier), the car's handsome aluminium coupé body appeared decidedly different to the regular Sports and, when completed in June '61, featured an 80bhp A-series lump. In the hands of Wing Commander McKenzie it proved a giant-slayer in club racing. A year later, a stage 3 Coventry Climax FEW unit was substituted, and the car never finished lower than third in its class during an extensive year-long race programme. But this attractive coupé would have been too expensive to build in volume, so the Turner-Alexander remained the sole example of its breed.

Jack Turner meanwhile had similar ideas for a coupé model. Fearing that Sports sales would flounder, he devised the GT as a fall back. Styled by Turner himself, this handsome machine took its public bow at the '62 London Racing Car Show (although it had been featured in the press a year earlier), and was well received. The basis was a glassfibre monocoque, with a steel floor bonded in with square-tube sections fore and aft. Front suspension was largely Triumph Herald derived, with a live rear axle located by trailing arms and a Panhard rod with telescopic dampers. Power came from a Ford 109E 1340cc 'four', or Coventry Climax's 1220cc FEW screamer, priced at £850 and £999 in kit-form respectively. Capable of 110mph, just nine of these handsome machines were made up until 1965, as Sports production took precedence.

Turner

Following the use of Ford's 1.5-litre pre-crossflow engine in late-model Sports MkIIs, this unit became standard equipment for the MkIII that emerged in late-'63. Visually unchanged, aside from a bonnet scoop and elliptical rear lights, it remained largely untouched until '66 when disaster struck: Jack Turner suffered a heart attack. With no company infrastructure to speak of, the firm was liquidated.

Turner had been involved in numerous projects at the time, including a twin-cam cylinder head for the BMC A-series engine, and a new, amorphous baby GT with Hillman Imp running gear. Although the hugely enthusiastic designer/engineer would recover in the fullness of time, he sadly never returned to manufacturing cars.

But the company's founder did inspire Turner devotee Mark Clarkson to develop his own take on the marque in the early '80s, with the MC Acer. A near-identical copy of a Sports Mk1, it was offered with a sturdy box-section chassis, and a choice of Vauxhall or Nissan running gear. Around a dozen were sold up until 1991, when the rights passed to Carlton Automotive which, at best, produced five more.

A Turner MkII with Alexander-tuned engine. Alexander's speciality was a BMC A-series with a crossflowed cylinder head.

The one and only alloy-bodied Alexander-Turner. This car proved a giant-slayer in club racing.

TVR

The Tuscan V8 superseded the Griffith in early 1967, using the same specification 195bhp and 271bhp engines as its forebear. *(Simon Clay)*

From little acorns do mighty oaks grow. Or rather from a lashed-together one-off special matures Britain's largest independent sports car manufacturer. With TVR's popularity presently running at an all-time high, with a bewildering array of models predominately powered by bespoke engines rather than mainstream producers' hand-me-downs, it is hard to believe that the Blackpool icon's origins were rather more modest. The marque has come a long way since Trevor Wilkinson built a special around the remains of an Alvis Firebird back in '47.

Having grown up around his family's pram distribution business in Blackpool, it was inevitable that Wilkinson would join the firm, but not before an apprenticeship with a local garage at the age of 14, back in '37. Turned down for service during World War II, Wilkinson managed the family business until '46 when, aged 23, he formed Trevcar Engineering in a converted wheelwright's workshop in nearby Beverley Grove. His father agreed to supply much-needed funds to furnish the tiny facility with equipment and, before long, Trevor was doing a roaring trade repairing cars. He also proved something of an inventor, devising arcade machines and a machine for coating chocolate onto cream eggs. But these acted as mere diversions as the young entrepreneur envisaged himself as a motor mogul.

On completing the Alvis Special, Wilkinson joined forces with Jack Pickard to form TVR Engineering, the former taking three initials from his Christian name for the tag. Converting decommissioned army lorries for civilian use provided enough finance to build another car. Two years of evenings and weekends were subsequently sunk into the project, neither partner being able to draw on any real automotive engineering expertise. It swiftly became a case

TVR 1800S	
Made	Blackpool, Lancashire
Engine	Front-mounted, water-cooled 1798cc ohv 'four'
Construction	Steel backbone chassis with glassfibre body
Top speed	110mph
0–60mph	8.6 seconds
Price new	£1120 (1966)

Early-'50s TVR special complete with RGS-derived bodyshell.

of trial and error. Wilkinson's design progressed through guesswork rather than premeditated ideals. What finally emerged in 1949 was a cigar-shaped, cycle-winged special with multi-tubular frame, independent trailing arm suspension, Morris 8 rear axle, an 1172cc Ford sidevalve 'four', and a rev counter sourced from a Spitfire fighter 'plane. Both partners were disappointed with their efforts, the diminutive sportster being sold to Wilkinson's cousin for £325.

Further specials were built along similar lines, but didn't prove financially viable. Crafting the alloy body, with all its double curvature, was laborious, and the body was expensive to produce so it was decided that future TVRs would feature glassfibre bodies. After looking at various proprietary bodyshells, the partners chose Dick Shattock's pretty RGS Atalanta coupé, modified to suit the shorter TVR wheelbase.

The TVR 'sporting saloon' was produced from '52 with largely Austin A40 running gear, and was offered in kit form for £650. Once completed, the factory claimed a top speed of 90mph and a 0–60mph time of an optimistic 13 seconds. Other engines could be accommodated, 1.5-litre MG TF and 2.5-litre Lea-Francis being used among others, while customers could purchase just the chassis for clothing in a body of their choice – Microplas and Rochdale being the most popular.

Among the many enthusiasts beating a path to TVR's door was American Oldsmobile dealer Ray Saidel. A keen amateur racer, he had found some

TVR's short-lived competition department readying Granturas for the disastrous 1962 Le Mans bid.

John Forrest about to spin his Grantura MkIIA in the Courtyard section of the Bo'ness Hillclimb, 1963.

The pretty Fiore-styled, steel-bodied Tina was named after TVR racer Gerry Marshall's daughter.

success campaigning an Allard J2 and, improbably, a pair of Dellow trials cars. One of these was subsequently re-bodied with an all-enveloping aluminium 'shell in an effort to make it lighter and more aerodynamic. But the Dellow chassis was just too heavy to ever be truly competitive, so Saidel approached TVR to build a new frame to his specifications. He requested it be fitted with a 1.1-litre Coventry Climax FWA engine mated to an MGA 'box with Volkswagen trailing arm suspension and steering.

Around this time, the firm had taken on Bernard Williams as director and sales manager. And it was he who persuaded Bolton businessman Fred Thomas to invest in the company. In '56, TVR Engineering took out a lease on a former brickworks in the Layton suburb of Blackpool. In June, Saidel took delivery of his chassis, having it clothed in an attractive alloy skin. After numerous handling problems, the Jomar, as it was dubbed, proved competitive in SCCA racing, prompting an order for two more cars. TVR similarly produced a handful of Jomars with glassfibre bodies for UK consumption.

Saidel was appointed as TVR's US distributor that same year, and prompted the new coupé body that would remain a constant for the next 20 years. Using two Microplas bonnets (one at the front, one at the back), a stumpy, closed notch-back sports car was created. Displayed at the '58 New York Motor Show, the newcomer was an instant hit, with 200 deposits taken before the event was over: a figure that the tiny Blackpool concern couldn't possibly cope with. The previous year, a variation on the theme made its official debut in the UK. The Grantura featured a tubular backbone chassis with Volkswagen-derived trailing arms and torsion bar suspension. With a body styled, for want of a better word, by Wilkinson and Pickard, it drew heavily on the previous coupé. Offered with a variety of engines including the asthmatic Ford sidevalve, MG and various Coventry Climax units, this peculiarly shaped sportster proved reasonably popular, but the firm had over-extended itself.

In December '58, TVR Engineering was officially liquidated, living to fight another day as Layton Sports Cars, with a sister company, Grantura Engineering, acting as components

Like its coupé sibling, the Tina roadster remained unique. Jensen and Aston Martin declined to take on production on TVR's behalf.

Martin Lilley's personal 271bhp Tuscan V8 being road-tested by *Motor* in 1967.

supplier from February '59. With a new team of directors, Grantura production gradually resumed, but delays had prompted a number of orders to be cancelled and Sadel's goodwill to ebb: he quit as US agent the following year.

The Grantura Mk2 arrived in 1960 with an evolved body style. The nose area featured two nostril-like air intakes, the rear wings extended into tiny, vestigial tailfins with new Lucas light clusters. Underneath, it was more of the same, but with stiffened-up suspension, and a rack-and-pinion steering arrangement offered on Coventry Climax-engined cars in place of the usual worm-and-sector set-up. In '61, the model featured further revisions, the Mk2A featuring Girling front disc brakes and Dunlop centre-lock wire wheels – all this for £880 in kit form.

But the marque remained on a knife-edge between prosperity and disaster. Arnold Burton, scion of the Leeds retail tailors, had sunk £3000 into Layton Sports Cars in 1960, but this was not enough, the auditor noting: 'Due to inadequate working capital, differences of opinion among directors, too rapid production and excessive wastage, I cannot view the company's future with any optimism.' A bleak forecast, but somehow the firm weathered the storm and, by this time, had managed to amass an astonishing ten directors. Wilkinson, meanwhile, was effectively ousted from any meaningful role by John Thurner, who had been installed to oversee TVR development.

Somehow, money was found for Thurner to produce an all-new chassis for the Grantura Mk3 of '61. Discernibly stiffer than the Wilkinson original, the new unit sported a wheelbase extended by ten inches, and a wider and taller transmission tunnel. The outriggers acted as mounting points for the bodyshell while serving as side impact protection. The suspension, too, was reworked, with a Triumph Herald-derived, TVR-modified front wishbone set-up.

In September of the same year, Aitchison-Hopton, a Chester sports car retailer, took a controlling interest in the firm, changing the company name to TVR Cars Ltd. Under this new regime, a number of new dealers were appointed, and sales increased dramatically. Then, the good work was thrown away with a disastrous foray into international motor sport. In January '62, former

BRM man and Standard-Triumph competitions manager Ken Richardson was hired to prepare a team of cars for an onslaught on blue-chip endurance classics, starting with the Sebring 12-hour race just seven weeks away. Three Grantura Mk2As were built with lightweight 'shells and Mk3 bonnets, powered by 1588cc MGA engines with HRG-crossflowed cylinder heads and twin 40DCOE Webers. During the race, two cars retired due to axle failure and engine breakages, although the Sagerman/Donohue entry lasted the distance, albeit way down the running order.

These race cars stayed in the US with new owners, while attention turned to Le Mans. But not before an attempt on the Tulip Rally which netted a third-in-class in a rather less trick Mk2A driven by Arnold Burton. For the French enduro, three cars were prepared from a £10,000 budget. All Mk3s, the three-car equipe were resplendent in white with two BRG stripes. Despite having a former event winner on the driving strength (Ninian Sanderson), the outing was to prove an unmitigated disaster. After numerous problems in practice, only one car made the start. Only fifteen minutes into the race, it retired with a blown head gasket. One final stab, in the Goodwood Tourist Trophy, saw the Keith Ballisat-driven car finish a lowly eleventh.

The financial drain of the racing programme, allied to the money sunk into an aborted Frank Costin-penned DKW-powered prototype, saw all of Aitchison-Hopton's good work undone. In April '62, an increasingly marginalised Trevor Wilkinson had left the firm for good, and in November, the doors of TVR Cars Ltd were closed with debts of £77,000. Grantura Engineering meanwhile, which had effectively acted as a tax dodge, took centre stage.

Under the aegis of the TVR liquidators, the firm took over production of the Grantura and even developed the car, with the 1798cc MGB-powered Grantura 1800S unveiled in November '63, production starting the following summer.

The Tuscan V8 had a higher-quality cockpit than its predecessor, complete with wooden dashboard. *(Simon Clay)*

A bare TVR Vixen S2 chassis on display at the '68 Earls Court Motor Show. The gentleman with the cigarette is Marcos founder Jem Marsh.

With its cropped Kamm tail and Mk1-Cortina tail-light clusters, it was markedly more attractive than its forerunners. And sharing the revised body style was the awesome Griffith, powered by a cast-iron 289cu in Ford V8.

This extraordinary device was the brainchild of American car dealer and race entrant Jack Griffith. Legend has it that future Indy 500 winner Mark Donohue was having some work done on his Grantura in Griffith's workshop, alongside a Shelby Cobra. Bored mechanics dropped the V8 into the TVR for a joke, but it prompted a proper conversion built by Griffith's chief engineer George Clark. Whatever the truth, very few changes were made to the car's running gear over the regular 1800S aside from wider wheels and a different exhaust.

When the Griffith was unveiled at the Boston Motor Show in '63, no mention was made of TVR. Dubbed the Griffith 200, there was almost overwhelming interest, and a deal was quickly thrashed out, with Grantura Engineering supplying rolling chassis for the engines to be fitted at Griffith's workshops. Offered in two states of tune, the 200 produced 195bhp at 4400rpm, the 400 boasting 271bhp at 6500rpm. The latter was supposedly capable of 165mph, and reportedly terrifying to drive.

And it was at this time that the TVR story took another turn. Embroiled in the Trident saga (recounted elsewhere), the firm was yet again suffering severe financial trouble. A US dock strike had caused a cash-flow problem for Jack Griffith and, consequently, Grantura Engineering, while any meagre profits had been thrown at the Trident prototypes. Events came to a head in the summer of '65, when minority shareholder Arthur Lilley offered to buy the company's assets and found himself owning a car factory. He put his 23-year-old son Martin in charge, who was to proffer much needed stability to the liquidation-prone concern.

A new company was formed, TVR Engineering, and while the creditors' demands were being dealt with, the Lilleys learned that Bill Last had done a deal to take over the Trident project. This was a bitter blow, as this Trevor Fiore-styled GT represented one of the main reasons for buying the firm in the first place. The Lilleys were undeterred, if embittered, and Grantura production was given a boost with the arrival of the 1800S Mk4, which featured a more opulent cabin and revised front suspension with Triumph TR4 uprights. With the Mk4 offered in kit form for £998 or complete for £1272, Martin Lilley realised that it was costing the firm around £1500 to build each car.

In an effort to broaden TVR's appeal, Lilley Jr. devised several new models. The Tina project (named after marque exponent Gerry Marshall's first daughter) originally called for an Austin 1800 chassis to act as a basis. But

The wild TVR SM (also known as Zante) was styled by Harris Mann, better known for the Triumph TR7.

stylist Trevor Fiore preferred the notion of a smaller car in similar vein to the Fiat 850 Spider. Two steel-bodied prototypes – a coupé and roadster – were built in '66 on Hillman Imp platforms, and displayed at the Turin Salon. But despite favourable reviews, the Tina never made production, as the factory was simply ill-equipped to make them. Jensen and Aston Martin were both approached to take on production on TVR's behalf, but declined. Lilley lost around £15,000 in development costs as a result.

Rather more successful was the Tuscan V8 that superseded the Griffith in early '67. Aside from its substantial bonnet bulge, there was little to tell it apart from its 1800S sister. Using the same specification 195bhp and 271bhp (Special Equipment model) engines as the Griffith, the new model differed from its forerunner in having a higher-quality cockpit, complete with attractive wooden dashboard. But it was too close in price to Jaguar's E-type, so just 28 found homes in the first six months of production. Criticisms in the motoring press centred on its tiny doors which made entry and exit a feat of physical dexterity (a problem on all models). TVR responded by lengthening the wheelbase to 90 inches, enabling longer doors, this variant bearing the LWB (long wheelbase) designation. A further variation was the Tuscan SE LWB, which featured a body widened by four inches with a smoother bonnet, different bumpers, and faired-in tail-lights.

But sales were still virtually non-existent: TVR needed a volume seller. Enter the Vixen in 1966. Visually identical to the 1800S, save for a flat air intake atop the bonnet, the major difference was the powerplant. Erratic supplies of MGB engines from BMC prompted a switch to the cheaper 1.6-litre, 88bhp Ford Cortina GT 'four' (although the first 12 cars featured MG lumps to soak up remaining stock). With a lower price of £998 in kit form, few punters cared that the extra weight scrubbed a few miles-an-hour off the top end (106mph, 0–60mph in 11 seconds).

By 1968, TVR was producing its glassfibre bodies in-house, the Vixen S2 introduced in '68 featuring the longer 90-inch wheelbase of its Tuscan big brother. Mindful of the perceived (and justifiable) reputation for the poor build-quality of past models, Martin Lilley went to great pains to improve matters. The S2's coachwork was thicker, with better panel fit. A major change was the move to bolting the body to the chassis rather than bonding it with glassfibre during the build phase.

Mechanical changes were minimal, primarily consisting of the adoption of a Triumph Vitesse differential, and a power hike to 92bhp. Styling changes consisted of a move to twin bonnet vents and MkII Cortina tail-lights. Inside, the driving position was a vast improvement thanks to the lower steering column, while the dashboard was even more comprehensively equipped, fronted by a leather-rimmed steering wheel.

Amazingly, TVR Engineering ended 1967 in the black, having made a £600 profit. Of the 200 or so Vixens made thus far, around 70 per cent went Stateside. And this was just the start of a remarkable recovery of the firm's fortunes. In 1969, around 300 cars left the production line, primarily for export but, in an effort to stimulate home sales, the Vixen's price dropped to £1150 fully built (from £1216). There were also the short-lived Sport and Super Sport options for those seeking a little more urge.

Part of this new found prosperity was prompted by the Tuscan V6 that went on sale in mid-'69. Lilley realised that there was a canyon-like gap between the 1.6-litre Vixen and full-on Tuscan V8, so this new model was designed to plug the gap. Powered by a 136bhp, 3-litre Ford V6, it combined the Vixen's frame with the V8 car's Salisbury differential. Priced at £1492 in DIY form or £1930 for the turn-key option, around two cars left Blackpool each week for the first six months before demand slowly ebbed.

The following year saw a further take on the Vixen theme, the S3, that, aside from the Capri-spec 1.6-litre engine and revised door window frames, was virtually indistinguishable from its predecessor, 165 finding homes in just 12 months. 1970 also saw the move to a new 28,000sq ft factory, in an effort to keep up with demand. Overseas markets were booming, Sweden being an unlikely source of many orders.

But there were problems. The Tuscan V6's Ford lump failed to meet US Federal emission laws, prompting the move to 2.5-litre Triumph straight-six power from '71. The newly dubbed 2500M was to act as a precursor to the M-series cars that were to sustain TVR through the '70s. The same year also saw the arrival of the 1300, a Vixen fitted with a 63bhp Triumph Spitfire 'four' and gearbox. Performance was at best sluggish (at worst downright slow), the Spitfire-engined Vixen being barely capable of 90mph. Not surprisingly, TVR's flirtation with the economy end of the market proved a disaster, with just 15 cars being sold in two years. But the final six 1300s had the distinction of using the new 'M' chassis. This new structure used a mixture of square and round-section tubing, and proved noticeably stiffer than previous frames.

The new chassis also served under the SM (or Zante) prototype displayed at the '71 New York Motor Show. Styled by Harris Mann (of Triumph TR7 infamy), and built by Specialist Mouldings of Huntington, this bold wedge-shaped hatchback bore hints of Lamborghini Espada, and pre-dated TVR's '80s Tasmin-range. Sadly, US distributor Gerry Sagerman took an instant dislike to the car's uncompromising silhouette, and the project was canned. Though initially a mock-up, the one and only SM was later fitted with a Triumph motor and used by Lilley as his personal transport.

The Vixen meanwhile soldiered on in yet another incarnation, the S4 of '72 being an interim model before the launch of new breed cars, using the new frame but with the existing bodyshell. A paltry 23 cars were sold, as by this time TVR were gearing up for production of the new breed, so the Vixen and Tuscan models went the way of the Dodo.

Aside from the odd factory fire, the imposition of VAT, industrial strife and Machiavellian power shifts among directors, TVR survived the '70s, eschewing the kit-car trade and moving increasingly upmarket. In the hands of the charismatic Peter Wheeler since '82, the marque is now a genuine threat to Porsche, Lotus et al, on the home front at least. Something that nobody would ever have suspected 50 years ago: least of all Trevor Wilkinson.

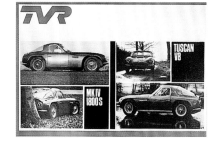

Unipower

The delectable A-Series-powered Unipower swiftly earned the moniker 'Mini Miura'.

The advent of the Mini in 1959 effectively spelt the end for the specials era. The Mini was relatively cheap, could seat four, and out-handle most contemporary sports cars. But, paradoxically, the Mini proved a highly popular base with the new generation of specialist car manufacturers, thanks to its simplicity and all-in-one running gear. While Butterfield, Gitane and Deep Sanderson were among the first to exploit Alec Issigonis's monobox as a source of inspiration, undoubtedly the best Mini-powered sporting chariot of the '60s was the low-flying Unipower.

Like so many low-volume sports cars, the concept was born out of a series of doodles and sketches penned on the backs of envelopes and newspapers. The man responsible for these jottings was Ernie Unger, a Ford development engineer and club racer. Having long admired Carlo Abarth's diminutive GTs, he harboured dreams of building similar machines in England, and a chance encounter at a Goodwood race meeting with old acquaintance Val Dare-Bryan in 1963 provided the impetus to turn this fantasy into reality.

Dare-Bryan was engaged in designing the improbably named Attila sports-racer for touring car ace Roy Pierpoint, and it was within his Surrey workshop that the as yet unnamed prototype GT began to take shape in the early months of 1965. Unger had already sketched out the basic concept, with Dare-Bryan concentrating on working drawings. As the desire was to use as many proprietary components as possible, to reduce tooling costs, the readily available BMC Mini A-series 'four' was chosen due to its availability, efficient packaging and endless tuning potential. Meanwhile, the pretty body was designed around an off-the-shelf Triumph Spitfire windscreen and steel

Unipower GT	
Made	Perivale, Middlesex
Engine	Mid-mounted, cast-iron 1275cc 'four'
Construction	Semi-spaceframe with glassfibre body
Top speed	106mph
0–60mph	9.5 seconds
Price new	£1150 (1967)

frame, by a moonlighting Ford stylist who was rumoured to have been involved in the GT40 project.

Two 'bedstead' chassis were completed not long after. The first was thrashed around Brands Hatch to test its worth, using the decrepit running gear of an old 850cc Mini van, while the second complete tubular frame was pieced together by Kingston upon Thames coachbuilder Robert Peel & Co. Wire was placed over the rolling chassis to plot the position of the car's silhouette and shut lines, a complete aluminium body being beaten out by hand.

With something approximate to a completed car, Unger and Dare-Bryan ran out of funds and began the search for an enthusiastic investor. Pierpoint expressed an interest, but couldn't raise the development capital, so Unger approached long-time friend and World Off Shore Powerboat Racing Champion, Tim Powell. When he wasn't playing with high-powered watercraft, Powell ran Universal Power Drives (UPD), manufacturers of forklift trucks and mechanical winches. The firm's sales executive was Andrew Hedges, a similarly daring bon viveur who, when he was not raging down the cresta run, could sometimes be found racing works Healeys at Le Mans. Despite being at odds with UPD's usual fare of industrial machinery, Powell and Hedges felt a small competition-inspired GT could bolster the company's image.

By November 1965, a small corner of UPD's Middlesex factory was set aside for the development and production of the diminutive sportster, now dubbed the Hustler GT. The aluminium-bodied prototype was dispatched to Specialised Mouldings for glassfibre bodies to be made. The car's tubular spaceframe, to which the reinforced nose section and bulkheads were bonded, was produced by Specialised Mouldings's neighbour Arch Motors. The BMC engines were swung through 180 degrees, and mounted on Mini front subframes just ahead of the rear axle line, retaining their transverse position. The gearchange operation was effectively inverted, with the gearlever mounted on the right-hand door sill, and the gate sporting a reversed shift pattern over a conventional Mini – first down towards the driver, second ahead, and so on. Suspension was independent all-round by double wishbones up front, with twin radius arms and single transverse links to the rear.

The Unipower's rear body panel tilted for access to the BMC A-series 'four'.

With the impending launch at the January '66 Racing Car Show, a change of name was deemed in order, despite the fact that publicity material had already been prepared. The Unipower (a contraction of Universal Power Drives) GT tag was chosen and, when the doors opened, the lithe two-seater was greeted with adulation from press and public alike. On display was a beautifully finished fixed-head coupé, along with a targa top variant. UPD took a number of advance orders, although it would be a further 12 months before production was in full swing. Just eight cars were delivered in '68,

Underneath the glassfibre skin, the Unipower featured a tough, thoughtfully conceived chassis.

causing many disgruntled customers to tire of waiting and cancel their orders.

Meanwhile, development continued apace in Middlesex. The lift-out targa top proved problematic in a rigid glassfibre structure, and was dropped, while the planned wind-up windows came to nothing, as cut-down sliding Mini affairs were adopted. Beneath the skin, the initial prototype's rear-mounted radiator proved totally inadequate, causing major overheating, so was repositioned down in the nose where it served dual functions – cooling the engine and heating the cockpit. Undeterred by the car's protracted birth, UPD returned to the Racing Car Show in 1967, with the Unipower now 'officially' on sale in component form for £950, with 998cc, 55bhp Cooper power and four-speed 'box, options including a sunroof, and a higher final-drive ratio along with a five-speed Jack Knight transmission. A hotter-still 1275cc-engined version was offered at £1150.

A full complement of Unipowers pictured outside the Universal Power Drives factory at Perivale.

With production underway, albeit at a rather leisurely pace, interest in the Unipower reached foreign parts. Although only one left-hand-drive car was built, UPD sold GTs overseas to countries as diverse as the USA, Hong Kong and Switzerland. One particular foreign customer, Gianfranco Padoan, personally collected his Unipower from Perivale before driving it back to his native Mestre. The Italian then restyled the car with rectangular headlights and a fussier hind treatment, marketing the car as the ESAP Minimach. After this aberration appeared in Italy's *Quattroroute* magazine, news reached Hedges, who flew out to see the car at the '68 Turin Salon and had it removed from the show. Following a brief legal battle, all publicity material was destroyed and Padoan and the Minimach were never heard of again.

Another distraction from the same year came courtesy of Quasar Khanh, a budding Vietnamese-born fashion designer, commissioned by a Paris-based textile firm to style a small batch of promotional vehicles. The result was the

The quite extraordinary Quasar-Unipower. Mercifully only six were built. The basis was a milk-float chassis.

The works Unipower awaiting shipping to Sicily for its ill-fated attempt at the Targa Florio.

faintly ridiculous Quasar-Unipower, a six-foot-high transparent cubist city car, with wall-to-wall sliding French windows and see-through inflatable seats. The basis was a cut 'n' shut milk-float chassis with 1098cc Mini power. Mercifully, only six cars were produced, all of them foisted on the French.

By November '68, just 60 Unipowers had been delivered. UPD's partners lost interest in building cars, passing on the project to aspiring racing driver Piers Weld-Forrester. The following month saw Dare-Bryan leave, with production shifting to a new North West London plant under the UWF (Unger, Weld-Forrester) Automotive banner, trading as Unipower Cars. At the '69 Racing Car Show, a revised MkII version was unveiled, key changes being softer-rate springing, different badging, and new tail-light clusters in place of the previous Vauxhall Viva HA units. The cabin also came in for a makeover, with repositioned instruments and a black padded fascia in place of the earlier anodised aluminium panel.

The new regime saw motor sport as a valuable publicity tool, and spent most of early '69 readying a lightweight car for long distance Group 6 events. Geoff Mabbs and John Miles had previously competed with some success in Janspeed-prepared, Cosworth FVA-engined cars, but this was a more serious effort with Le Mans the primary goal. Once completed, the works lightweight was entered in the Targa Florio, and with UPD man Andrew Hedges behind the wheel, the Unipower was a highly commendable twelfth fastest overall around the Sicilian circuit in practice. Sadly, it failed to start, as a mechanic had an off-road excursion at 4am on the morning of the race. UWF's Le Mans foray later that year proved equally disastrous. Despite being clocked at over 135mph down the Mulsanne Straight in practice, thanks to a 1340cc motor prepared by BMC's Competition Department, the car failed to make the cut.

The high costs of motor racing ultimately caused the Unipower's downfall. Road car development had ground to a resounding halt as the doomed competition programme took precedence, and inevitably production began to falter. Operations ceased in December '69, and UWF was wound up the following month having built only 15 cars. With the demise of Unipower died the possibility of producing the Bohanna Staples Diablo concept car that ultimately became the AC 3000ME.

While the paltry figure of just 75 cars doesn't sound overly impressive, the Unipower's influence was far reaching, and is still being felt in the specialist car industry today. And while the concept of Mini packaging with a pretty wrapper wasn't particularly original, Unipower's take on the theme was, and remains, the best yet.

Each of the eleven WSM Sprites made were individually coachbuilt by Peels of Kensington. No body moulds or jigs were ever made.

Douglas Wilson-Spratt never really intended becoming a motor manufacturer and, considering the meagre number of cars he built, some would argue that he never did. But this is to denigrate the efforts of a charming and hugely capable man, who's toe-in-the-water enterprise never extended to full immersion.

While the first WSM Sprite was completed in 1962, its design philosophy can be traced back to a Bentley special Wilson-Spratt built during the '50s, while running caravan maker Marlborough, having left the Bristol Car Company. After owning a series of vintage Bentleys, he gathered all the components to build the ultimate example. Using a chassis shortened and modified by Buckler man George Burton, this rakish machine was clothed in aluminium over a steel frame. Displaying what was to become a characteristic of all his designs, it was brimful of weight-saving details such as the side-lights made of alloy, or the skimpy, quick-release wings. This, the first of his many specials, was reportedly capable of topping 130mph, yet good for 20mpg.

In 1954, Wilson-Spratt tired of the largely seasonal caravan industry, and bought an Austin franchise in Leighton Buzzard. Delta Garages swiftly became the platform for a decade of amateur motor sport, mostly with Triumph TRs until Wilson-Spratt got wind of the impending Austin-Healey Sprite, and pressured BMC into letting him have one of the first three off the production line. Wilson-Spratt had the distinction of winning the first ever event for a Sprite, a minor Sporting Owner Drivers' Club rally, a month before the car's official announcement. Though initially Wilson-Spratt could barely contain his disdain for the car, he soon warmed to BMC's baby and entered the '59

WSM Sprite	
Made	Leighton Buzzard, Bedfordshire
Engine	Front-mounted, water-cooled 1098cc ohv 'four'
Construction	Unitary steel with alloy outer skin
Top speed	115mph (est)
0–60mph	8 seconds (est)
Price new	N/A (all cars built to order)

The WSM was conceived by Douglas Wilson-Spratt (seen here), and was originally intended as a one-off for his own competition use.

Monte Carlo Rally, retiring when a fanbelt broke and discovering that the spare was the wrong size.

By this time he had become thoroughly enamoured of the Sprite, and began doodling coupé versions. But they were, initially at least, to remain just sketches as he bought a Speedwell Sebring Sprite instead. However, he was not above tampering with its styling, adding Rolls-Royce tail-lights and a boot lid so that he could access the spare wheel more easily. After driving the car in the '62 Monte Carlo Rally, he joined forces with Jim McManus to form the Healey Centre in Swiss Cottage, London. And then followed what was to become the inspiration for the WSM series. The firm's works foreman, Peter Jackson, owned an alloy-bodied Sprite, and wanted a lightweight coupé body. Wilson-Spratt concocted new fastback bodywork built by Peels of Kingston (the small Surrey concern known for its work with Lotus and Brabham) under his direction, with a proprietary Speedwell bonnet added to keep costs down.

Suitably inspired, Wilson-Spratt set to work designing his own car along similar lines. Intended as a one-off for personal competition use, the first WSM (Wilson, Spratt, McManus) proved ultra lightweight, its aluminium body boasting a spaceframe structure at the rear to save on unnecessary poundage, pre-dating Healey's own efforts by some years. Weighing in at 10cwt (compared to the standard car's 13.5cwt), it was also strong, thanks to an integral rollover bar, a feature common to all subsequent 'Wuzzums'. Typical of his 'no compromise' approach, Wilson-Spratt refused to design the car around a windscreen – unlike many of his contemporaries – instead having a bespoke curved 'screen made by Tudor Glass. The car was entered for the '63 Monte Carlo Rally, where it proved fast but fragile, failing to last the distance.

The WSM Healey 3000 was supposedly good for 140mph but suffered from front end lift. The resemblance to the Ferrari 250 GTO can be seen here.

On the WSM's completion in October 1962, reaction from a highly complementary *Autosport* article saw Wilson-Spratt inundated with requests for replicas, and all thoughts of the car remaining unique evaporated. Two American customers decided that they wanted WSMs, stating that they could find homes for more cars in the States. So eleven WSM Sprites were made, the last in '66, at £450 for the lightweight Sprint edition, with standard GT versions costing £375. Some were alloy-bodied, another pair sporting glassfibre shells with aluminium doors. No two cars looked alike, the bonnets in particular subtly different on later cars. Wilson-Spratt was never entirely happy with the nose area, and went through three designs before being satisfied with his efforts. No body moulds or jigs were ever made, as Wilson-Spratt had never envisaged the demand for the car, so each was coachbuilt by Peels of Kingston.

Next up was a WSM-bodied Austin-Healey 3000, built in 1965 for racer Malcolm Bridgeland, who had comprehensively restyled his car against Silverstone's pit wall. Rather than rebuild it to original configuration, he commissioned Wilson-Spratt to re-clothe the car in an aerodynamic, all-enveloping alloy shell. With its long, curvaceous nose and stubby Kamm-tail rear, it resembled Ferrari's all-conquering 250GTO, at least in profile. The new, streamlined bodywork, with its integral spare-wheel hatch, was good for an additional 12mph over the standard car, although it apparently suffered chronic front-end lift around its 140mph top end.

On relocating from London to new premises in Leighton Buzzard, Bedfordshire, next came the WSM 1100, based on an MG 1100 floorpan, with a Mini Cooper S 1275cc A-series engine. The idea behind the project was

The WSM MGB was extensively campaigned in club events in the late '60s with some success.

to deliver 100mph while still recording 30–35mpg. The entire centre section of the donor car remained intact, with a new nose added, vaguely similar in appearance to the Ferrari 275GTB, along with a bulky Kamm tail. The result was not entirely happy looking, being rather ill-proportioned. Wilson-Spratt was unconcerned, as the 1100 more than achieved his goals. And despite being conceived as a road car, he campaigned the car with some success in minor MG Car Club events. Intended from the outset as a one-off for personal use, there was never any talk of building copies, not that Wilson-Spratt was inundated with requests for replicas.

Another non-WSM designated project from this time was a Jaguar XK150 shooting-brake built at the behest of VSCC man Douglas Hull. Showing typical attention to detail, the car featured built-in mounting points for a roof rack, so Hull could carry body panels around. Amazingly, the shooting-brake proved faster than the original open car, thanks to its superior aerodynamics.

The final WSM emerged in 1967. Built on the hull of a tuned MGB, it was made for Wilson-Spratt's son-in-law Mike Lewis (who had previously hillclimbed a WSM Sprite) and drew on established styling themes, only this time with a hatchback. This was arguably Wilson-Spratt's finest design, a heady mixture of Italianate delicacy of line with British brutishness. The results were light years away from the MG original, and a rival for anything produced by the Latin styling houses of the time. Displaying a remarkable turn of speed and admirable crash resistance, it beat ace-tuner Bill Nicholson's previously unbeaten 'B' and, when later fitted with a standard engine, could record 40mpg. Sadly, there was to be no production run, despite considerable demand. The one and only WSM B was subsequently sold on, and competed irregularly in club events before disappearing from view for several years. Today, it is back in the hands of its creator.

The WSM MGB was later rebuilt as a pure road car (despite racing roundels) and is now owned by its creator, Wilson-Spratt.

Regulations for sports car racing changed dramatically towards the end of the '60s, requiring hundreds rather than a handful of models to be built in order to be eligible, a requirement which Wilson-Spratt had no desire to conform with. Suffering from back problems exacerbated by his rallying exploits, Wilson-Spratt called it quits in '67, uprooting to the Isle of Man to set up an aircraft repair business. But, despite a long spell away from building cars, the hunger never altogether left him. He is currently threatening to revive the WSM Sprite, and has mooted a high-performance three-wheeler with plastic wings and fuselage-like body.

WSM

144

Butterfield

The Mini is often sited as prompting the downfall of the specials movement. Cheap, a keen handler and eminently tuneable, who would want a leaky, poorly engineered plastic contraption when they could have one of Alec Issigonis's cheeky little saloons? But it wasn't long before specialist car manufacturers took a closer look at this miniature shopping car. And the appallingly named Butterfield Musketeer had the dubious distinction of being the world's first ever kit car to be based on Mini running gear.

Produced by Butterfield Engineering of Nazeing, Essex, this unfortunate contraption was doomed from the outset. Launched at the '61 London Racing Car Show, it was one of the undoubted duds of the event: this lamentable device was utterly hideous. Riding on tiny ten-inch wheels, it appeared over-bodied, the tall A-series engine necessitating an elevated bonnet line with massive overhang. But though a riot of horrid proportions, the Musketeer was at least well equipped.

Butterfield offered the Musketeer in two forms, the 850 and 1000, both with brand new Mini powerplants and mechanics, mounted in a tough, multi-tubular semi-spaceframe chassis. The bodyshell featured a flip-up bonnet for easy engine access, while Koni adjustable shock absorbers featured on the options list. The cabin was more thoughtfully conceived than the exterior, with an attractive plank-like dashboard home to such novelties as a rev counter. The car even had two-speed windscreen wipers.

The strangely proportioned
Butterfield Musketeer at
the 1962 Racing Car Show.

But the biggest flaw in the plan was the car's price. At £848, it cost nearly twice as much as a Mini – and you had to build it. No great surprise then that, despite being offered until 1963, just three takers were persuaded to part with their hard-earned cash. It was left to subsequent Mini-based specialist cars such as the Unipower and Cox GTM to show how to do the job properly. Perhaps mercifully, there are no known Musketeer survivors.

Camber

CHECKPOINT INTRODUCE THE Camber GT

Derek Bishop was one of the early instigators of the specials boom with his pretty Heron 'shells that proved instantly popular with '50s kit-car builders. But after his bold attempt at moving upmarket with the Heron Europa proved a disaster, he joined forces with George Holmes to build an entirely new car, the Camber GT. The prototype was completed in 1966, this distinctive machine being jointly styled by the partners. Once the first bodyshell was completed in Bishop's Greenwich garage, it was transported to Holmes's Camber Sands, Sussex facility for the mechanical components to be fitted.

The GT's ill-formed glassfibre body was mounted on a square-tube semi-spaceframe chassis with Mini front and rear subframes. The silhouette was to some extent dictated by the lofty Mini A-series engine, which necessitated the elevated bonnet line. The Camber used the ten-inch wheels from the donor Mini, and this gave the impression that the car had an overly large body. The exposed door hinges and sliding side windows only served to heighten the car's rather basic image.

Making its first public appearance at the '67 Racing Car Show, this 2+2 was marketed under the Checkpoint banner. A semi-works car was entered in a number of events that season, with negligible success. The partnership between Bishop and Holmes soon soured, after just six cars had been sold. Holmes effectively took over the project and revised the car for '68, the most obvious change being the raised headlights (the original positioning was illegally low) which did nothing for the car's already unhappy visage.

Renamed the Maya GT, just six more cars were completed before Holmes's tragic death in a road accident. The moulds then moved on to a new home, but nothing more was ever heard.

Those who also served

A Camber GT in action on the track. The exposed door hinges are clearly visible.

The unfinished Dial Buccaneer debuted at the '71 London Racing Car Show.

Dial

The concept of the Dial Buccaneer was right on the money – a two-seater mid-engined road racer with the choice of either Ford pushrod or Lotus twin-cam 'fours'. Unfortunately, the execution of the concept was poor. Designed by Frank Sheen, and derived from an earlier autocross special, this awful device appeared in 1970, before making its public debut at the '71 London Racing Car Show to deafening silence. Unfinished, with a poorly shaped, badly moulded glassfibre body that lacked a windscreen, it redefined the word 'unprofessional'.

The basis was a tough, square-section steel spaceframe chassis, with all-round independent suspension derived from the Triumph Spitfire. The engine of choice was mounted in-line, amidships, with power running through a Volkswagen gearbox and final drive as supplied by Grays, Essex-based Dial Plastics. The dramatic, if rather oddly shaped bodyshell incorporated aluminium reinforcement at key stress areas. Tipping the scales at just under 10cwt, the promotional material claimed an optimistic top speed of 110mph, and 0–60mph in less than 10 seconds, with just a 1.1-litre Ford Escort 'four' providing power.

Amazingly, production reached double figures, later cars featuring larger gullwing doors and deeper windscreens. The car was offered as late as 1975, when Dial Plastics went bust. For all the dubious build quality, the Buccaneer was apparently a fine-handling car, and one example, known as the Ceja Twin-Cam, found great success in hillclimbing during the early '70s, using Piper-modified, 1860cc Ford power (not a twin-cam engine confusingly). The last example made took its owner three years to complete, and featured a lightweight aluminium spaceframe, with power provided by a Lotus twin-cam with a stage 3 cylinder head.

Emery

Paul Emery was one of only two men to make cars which complied with each of the first four World Championship formulae from 1950–'65. The other was Enzo Ferrari. Emery not only designed and built his own cars, but raced them as well. Unfortunately, he never had the necessary finance to back up his engineering skills, and was unable to exploit the full potential of his designs. His brush with the road car market was similarly cash strapped. From his West London workshop, Emery conceived the Emery GT in 1963, the first of a number of specialist sports cars to use the Hillman Imp as a basis.

A bulbous, oddly proportioned machine, the GT featured a spaceframe chassis with its glassfibre body bonded on. The front end was suspended by tubular wishbones, and the engine was mounted virtually amidships, just in front of the rear axle. The gearbox was inverted and located behind the power unit, to lower the centre of gravity and aid weight distribution. Tipping the scales at just over 10cwt, this featherweight coupé proved a giant-killer in racing, John Markey taking 15 class wins from 16 outings during the '63 season, including two overall wins.

But as a road car, the GT wasn't even remotely refined, build quality a seemingly alien concept. When a visitor to the '63 Racing Car Show casually commented that the door on one side was deeper than the one on the other, Emery retorted: 'Does it matter? You can only see one side at a time.' Just four cars were made, the alloy-bodied prototype serving as a basis for the glassfibre moulds used for production 'shells. One car was subsequently exported to America, another to Germany. Emery later built 12 Hillman Imps with four-inch roof chops and heavily tuned engines, before turning to Midget oval-racer manufacture, the only motor sport arena from which he ever made any money.

Futura

Robin Stratham had already found some measure of commercial success with his Mini Jem kit car (a pretty derivative of the DART that also spawned the Mini Marcos) when he unveiled the extraordinary Futura at the '71 Racing Car Show. Although only a wooden mock-up, this wonder-wedge proved the undoubted star of the event, and provided Stratham's Fellpoint concern with a rush of orders. When the definitive prototype was completed a few months later, it was greeted with a mixture of awe and crushing disappointment. The glassfibre body, styled by Stratham himself, was brimming with novel features, not least the vast windscreen which doubled as a door; to enter the cabin you simply walked in from the leading edge of the nose. On the reverse side of the dashboard sat a bank of four headlights that ultimately proved

The Futura's styling was striking, but humble Volkswagen Beetle running gear lay underneath.

148

illegal, prompting more conventional units to be housed in the dramatically scalloped wings. But if the Futura's styling was strikingly innovative, the underpinnings were anything but. The basis for the exotic-looking GT was nothing more than a Volkswagen Beetle (for which the brochure apologised), although production cars were promised with more suitable running gear.

But the Futura never reached the production stage. Developing the car had overstretched Statham financially, and the pauperised Fellpoint crashed in July '71. Just three Futuras had been made, one going to Persia which, thanks to the country's crippling 200 per cent import tax, cost around £12,000. The final example was shipped to Brazil in several pieces as 'industrial parts' to avoid import duty. Plans to produce the car in South America ultimately came to nothing. The original 1.2-litre flat-four Veedub-powered prototype did the usual show tours until the end of the decade before disappearing from view.

Ikenga

The radical Ikenga, based on a McLaren M6 Can-Am chassis, caused a sensation when it was unveiled to the media.

Specialist sports car are by definition a little out of the ordinary, but few can equal the ill-fated Ikenga for dramatic effect. The brainchild of American-born designer David Gittens, this beautifully crafted, low-slung supercar looked for all the world as though it had wandered off the set of some low-budget B-movie when it debuted at Harrods in 1968. Built by ace panel beaters Williams & Pritchard, and engineered by Elva man Ken Sheppard, the basis for this extraordinary machine was a McLaren M6 Can-Am chassis with a Chevrolet Camaro-sourced 5.3-litre V8 driving through a five-speed ZF 'box. The dramatic silhouette was continuously refined prior to making its public debut, the original forward-hinging canopy replaced by a more attractive one-piece front section made by Radford. Only the awkward-looking scoop atop the rear deck interrupted an otherwise attractive silhouette. Inside, the car was equally radical. Among the (possibly bogus) fixtures and fittings were a bank of fluid-filled instruments and assorted fairy lights. There was also a distance proximity sensor, rear view TV camera for ease of parking, and a Perspex boot lid that doubled as an air brake.

At its unveiling, the Ikenga caused a furore, the media shifting into hyperbole overload, waxing lyrical of Britain's answer to the Lamborghini Miura. Optimistic performance figures suggested a 162mph top speed, and 0–100mph time of 11.5 seconds, and there was even talk of a limited production run of 50 cars. But precisely where Gittens expected to lay his hands on so many McLaren chassis remains a mystery.

Ultimately, the Ikenga (which translates to a two-horned mythical beast or a man's 'life force' depending on who you believe) remained unique. Nobody coughed up the £9000 asking price, and Gittens moved on to other projects. After a brief spell at Radford, he returned to America, leaving the one and only prototype behind.

Peel

The Isle of Man isn't famous for its automotive industry, but Manx-based Peel Engineering were, for nearly two decades, embroiled in a number of unusual and often frivolous projects. The firm found fame, and a certain notoriety, for

The Peel Trident Mini was redubbed the Viking Minisport after the project passed to Bill Last's company.

its micro-cars, the first being the rather crude Manxman, a three-wheeler with rotating doors. But sports cars were the major draw and, after numerous false dawns, the tiny concern introduced the P1000 in 1955. Designed to fit on an unmodified Ford E93A chassis, it wasn't exactly a vision of loveliness and was soon dropped.

The P1000 was followed by an all-glassfibre Mini, and numerous micro-cars, before the Peel Trident Mini was introduced in 1966. An extremely ugly machine, this kit-form coupé used Mini subframes and an A-series engine mounted on a square-tube perimeter chassis. Clothing the frame was a glassfibre body with the donor car's windscreen and modified doors. Notable for little other than the fact that it was a full four-seater, the Trident was priced at £230 for a bare 'shell. Launched at that year's London Racing Car Show, just two were made before the project passed to TVR dealer Bill Last's company, Viking Performance of Suffolk. Last had found meagre success with his rag-top Wolseley Hornet conversion, and hoped for more luck from the newly redubbed Viking Minisport. An extensive racing programme was rewarded with precious few results, but Last promoted the car heavily, and a further 22 were sold that year. However, he had become embroiled in the Trident saga (see elsewhere) and, as the Minisport became increasingly marginalised, it was dropped altogether in early '67. Peel Engineering survived the '60s by turning to the production of industrial mouldings, an infinitely more profitable business than car manufacture.

Quest

The Quest story is as implausible as it is comical. Originally conceived by Gerry Anderson, three of these Derek Meddings-styled machines were constructed in 1968 as mere props for the movie *Doppelganger*. Built under the direction of works Ford entrant Alan Mann (who was also responsible for *Chitty-Chitty-Bang-Bang*), these suitably space-age vehicles proved an effective disguise for the Ford Zephyr running gear (and 1.6-litre Cortina engine) underneath. The fakery extended inside the cockpit, home to a bewildering array of 'nuclear-drive' warning lights and switches, none of which served any purpose.

While filming on location, one visitor to the set was Sidney Carlton who subsequently persuaded friend David Lowes to stump up the cash to put the vehicle into production. The Explorer Motor Company was formed, and £25,000 invested, for want of a better word, in development, including the manufacture of fresh moulds. The plan was to buy brand new Zephyrs and

The Quest was used as Commander Straker's personal transport in the '70s *UFO* TV series.

plonk the glassfibre 'shells on them, the resulting four-seater to be known as the Quest.

Offered for public consumption with a lofty £3000 price tag, a few additional gimmicks were thrown into the mix in order to entice prospective owners into parting with their cash. These included fibre-optic cables connected from the lights to the dash' to reassure the driver that they were working (!) and a 'guaranteed harmless' radio-active gas-filled fascia to provide 24-hour illumination.

Unsurprisingly, by 1970 the firm had received no orders and folded. But that wasn't altogether the end of the story. The Mann-built cars were bought by Pinewood Studios for use in the *UFO* TV series where they were piloted by mop-haired Commander Straker (Ed Straker). Once the programme was cancelled, one example went to DJ, Dave Lee Travis. And, amazingly, all still exist, albeit in derelict condition.

Siva

The rectangular steering 'wheel' and unusually sited instruments can be seen in this interior view of a Siva S350.

Neville Trickett was one of Britain's most consistently adventurous car designers from the mid-'60s through to the late-'80s. A successful amateur saloon car racer in machines as diverse as Mini Coopers and Isuzu Bellets, he had already conceived the delightful Mini Sprint, and rather less lovely Opus HRF, before introducing the first model in the Siva series in 1969. Over the ensuing five years, it seemed as though barely a month passed without him launching yet another car, only to lose interest when it was completed. These often bizarre contraptions included VW and Ford E93A-based Edwardian-style horseless carriages, Mini-powered buggies and utility vehicles and, most adventurous of all, the S530.

Commissioned by *The Daily Telegraph* for its stand at the November '71 Earls Court Motor Show, the S530 prototype was completed in just four months. Powering this wedge-shaped projectile was a 5340cc Aston Martin V8 which, according to the publicity material, meant a top speed of

The Siva S530 was commissioned by *The Daily Telegraph* for its stand at the '71 Earls Court Motor Show.

180mph, and 0–60mph in less than five seconds. Unusual features abounded, not least the use of a rectangular steering 'wheel', and a bank of instruments concealed behind a Perspex nacelle, plus electrically operated gullwing doors.

Aston Martin expressed an interest in taking over the project, borrowing the car for evaluation, but it wasn't in the best of financial health at the time, so the interest soon waned. Favourable press reports prompted Trickett to attempt a production run with lightly revised styling and small-block Chevrolet V8 power, but other, less exotic, Siva projects soon took precedence. The marque lingered on until the late-'70s, when Trickett turned to the more profitable arena of hovercraft manufacture. The one and only S530 has since disappeared.

Voodoo

Geoff Neale and John Arnold originally planned to build a brace of Voodoos, one each, as a purely private venture. But this alluring design was too good not to share. A beautifully crafted, superbly executed machine, it is hard to believe that it was the work of just two men beavering away in a Coventry lock-up. Making its public debut on the stand of *The Daily Telegraph* at the '71 Earls Court Motor Show, the car on display was little more than a mock-up. But it wowed the crowds, appearing in numerous magazines and at other events while the partners set to work on the definitive Voodoo.

The Voodoo appeared at the '73 London Racing Car Show, and with its tuned Imp Sport all-alloy 'four' was capable of over 115mph.

With backing from an enthusiastic businessman, the partners finished a running prototype the following year. To ensure structural integrity, the car's glassfibre body was bonded to its spaceframe chassis, the nose and tail sections being bolted on. The entire rear section flipped up, as did the canopy section, while the impossibly curvaceous windscreen was a Chevron B16 item. By the time it appeared at the '73 London Racing Car Show, the car's specification was complete, including a 998cc Imp Sport all-alloy 'four' with a hot cam and performance exhaust. Weighing just 11cwt and with 90bhp on tap, the Voodoo could top 115mph. The front end was suspended by a Vauxhall Viva-derived double wishbone arrangement, the entire Imp rear end being used with adjustable shockers, and the Voodoo was reportedly a tenacious handler.

But, just as the car's future seemed assured, the backing was withdrawn and Arnold was tragically killed in a car crash. A third Voodoo was under construction at the time. The project was soon canned, but Neale planned a revival in the early '80s. Sadly, it never materialised.